CROSSING THE THRESHOLD

METAPHORS OF AN EVOLVING FAITH

A MEMOIR

" Growing up is optional.
Growing old is mandatory"
Your wisdom gets you through.

HARLENE WALKER

(ch. Letting Go pg 13
    Going Beyond pg 99)

Shalom Harley.
                2024

Produced by:

FriesenPress

Suite 300 — 852 Fort Street
Victoria, BC, Canada V8W 1H8
www.friesenpress.com
Distributed to the trade by The Ingram Book Company

Table of Contents

Dedicated to:
My mother, Dorothy Elizabeth May Hind 1911 — 2005.
Who at age 93 said,
"It's time that this is said.
So many of us think it but no one has said it."

My husband, Ross James Walker —
Who when I entered seminary said,
"For 25 years you supported me in my career,
for the next 25 years I will support you in your career."

I am thankful for their commitment and accompaniment.

At the beginning of her book, *Crossing the Threshold*, Harlene Walker writes about being a member of a small study group some years ago. The group, in which I also participated, was formed at a time of intense faith questioning in the church. In her deeply personal book, Harlene describes how her journey has continued through the years. For all of us, her story is a reminder that the faith quest, wherever it may take us, is a lifelong journey. In the words of J.R.R. Tolkien, "The road goes forever on and on".

Rev. Dr. Gordon J. Freer, ON. friend and crosser of many thresholds (silent generation)

ACKNOWLEDGEMENTS

I am indebted to the men and women who graciously and continually received me during every stage of this evolving faith crossing. My family, relatives, and many friends formed a wide circle around me. Within the bigger circle are several smaller circles.

Twelve years ago a circle of four women read my original, poorly written chapters. Thank you Diana Habkirk, Beth Harlow, June Maffin and Shirley Thompson; you saw past the potholes and rocks on the road to the topic, an idea whose time had come. Diana, you, became the compass who kept me focused and on track. I appreciate your tenacity that got me to this page.

To my circle of soul sisters, Edith Baird, Patti Gunning, Mary Leslie, Barb Quinn and Lyn Robertson, thank you for guiding me with your wisdom and encouragement.

Now I know why every book must have an editor. Anne Le Dressay smoothed out the edges in my writing and made me think twice about how to write what I wanted to say. Thank you.

In the chronos time of finishing this project, each of you in the wider circle gifted me with invaluable help, and always at the opportune, kairos time. For this I am grateful.

AN INVITATION

My changing faith-life engaged me in taking a spiritual hike through forest trails.

The forest is my cathedral. Its canopy forms a domed, stained glass window. The floor varies from crispy leaves, soft moss and evergreen needles to hard grey rock. The pews can be a smooth-surfaced, debarked, fallen tree, or a large boulder.

At any time, it is open and ready to receive me, while all day long a choir performs its anthems. The soprano voices of birds calling, the bass voice of the wind blowing from far away and drawing slowly near, the constant mantra of the squirrels' chit-chatter, the branches rustling, and the leaves crunching underfoot, accompany me on my walk. Or I listen to the silence interrupted only by the solo voice of a creaky tree swaying to and fro. All of it is my sanctuary. It is the place where I am able to feel, to ponder, to exercise, to enjoy a friend's company, to partake of the common meal. Or I can yell like Tarzan, sing off-key, whistle a happy tune and talk to myself out loud.

As I review this spiritual journey, I invite you to hike along the trails with me.

INTRODUCTION

When this Current Era turned 2000 years old and we all celebrated the entrance of the second millennium, my husband and I were having dinner in the home of close friends. Chatting after dessert, I casually mentioned that we were considering not attending church any more. I said that worship, as we experienced it, was irrelevant to our lives, and that likely the church would have to die before it became relevant. The hostess looked at me, quite shocked,

"That would be terrible if there was no more church!" she gasped.

"Why would it make any difference to you?" I replied, "You never go to church anyway."

Silence.

"You know, you're right," she answered. "I never thought about it, but I guess I wouldn't miss it."

The tradition of one generation following in the religious and spiritual footsteps of the preceding generation has fallen on fallow ground.

Ushering in the 1900s a new generation born 1901 -1924, designed and built a modern society, from horse and carriage to horseless carriage. This great generation was followed by the Silents (1925-1942), who were "seen and not heard" yet compassionate and liberal. The idealistic Boomer generation (1943-1960) gave us new visions which radically deconstructed our lifestyles. Their motto was "You build it up, mother, we gonna tear it down." Next the alienated Gen Xers (1961-1981), disillusioned but pragmatic, reacted with their motto, "Whatever works." Ushering in this millennium, the Gen Y or Millennial generation (1981-2001) brought a hopeful, caring attitude to our society. More privileged than any other North American generation, their motto — "We can do it, and we don't need your help" (Mabry, 2012, pp. 13-22) — indicated to our world that they not only could master technological advances but also solve our problems. The church was just one more institution that was not part of their vocabulary. From my perspective, a disconnect developed between those Christians in the pews and those post-Christians who are anywhere but in the pews. However, it is not the empty pew that concerns me. It is the situation of so many who have disconnected from the spiritual side of their life. They are healthy in body (physically fit), healthy in mind (emotionally stable), but the un-nurtured spirit is truncated.

As I unfold my spiritual life here, I wish to connect with you who grew up prior to the Boomers when spirituality was thought of differently than it is in this millennium; I hope to connect with you Boomers moving into retirement, who may have more time to ponder things spiritual; also, I admire you who are independent, technologically savvy Millennials, new to the notion of holy ground, yet who recognize the sacredness of spiritual energy.

During years of experiencing God in my life, I have learned to listen and to respond to the spirit's nudging, which brings me to the reason why I decided to write about the changes in my Christian faith and the evolution of my spirit. For the last 30 years, I have recorded these experiences in my journals. Journal writing is an individual activity, a reflection on life. My soul friend gave me my first journal, and in it she inscribed these words:

May this journal, for your reflections, thoughts, anxieties, concerns and hopes, be a place for you to search, to wonder, to pray, to marvel … to be aware of God's continuing presence in your life.

From that first day of writing back in 1984, I made the decision to keep the journal solely about the soul; it has become a continuing sacred presence in my life, just as she had suggested. Therefore my writings are original, inspired, written-from-the-heart reflections on, and reactions to, what I have just been feeling, or thinking or reading.

Over the years they have created a spiritual trail of the evolutionary stages en route.

This book is a story *about* spirituality, not a description of *how* to be spiritual. Each chapter begins with a metaphor for the journey; it is followed by an account of my own learning and experiences, and then ends with my free verse style poetry. In the Appendix there is an opportunity for you to connect your story with mine by following the prompts in the section, "Interacting with the Memoir." As well, there is a factual chronology of my life. While my spiritual journey will be very different from your spiritual journey, I believe that we each are entrusted with spirit energy, and that we are empowered to develop its potential within us. I think of my spiritual growth as the evolution of my faith–life, which has been lived within the faith ground of Christianity.

But first I must make a disclaimer. I am neither theologian nor academic. I am a retired ordained woman in the United Church of Canada (UCC). I am a grandma looking for spiritual nourishment. I hope that you can review your own spirituality as you read about my spirituality. It is one that is grounded, but not stuck, in religion.

From My Journal

The Trinity

I.
Holy Spirit, Jesus, God
Three Two One
One God yet Three.
Who are you?
Where are you?
Beyond in my midst why
Western God transcendent
Eastern God so personal?
Think Feel
Rational reasoning
Experiential feeling
II.
God, depth of my being
God does not exist
God is.
Jesus, paradigm of humanity
Jesus a man, a myth
Jesus is.
Holy Spirit, Soul-Bridge
Holy Spirit does not exist
Holy Spirit is.
III.
Sacred loving energy
courageous, strong, compassionate, creating
empowering, encouraging, giving, listening, accepting,
the ground of all being.
Sacred loving energy is.
April 1983

"Be still and know that I am God
Be still and know that I am
Be still and know
Be still
Be." (Psalm 46:10)

Along the reading trails you will come upon a blank page.
This space is for your Personal Notes and Reflections.

The dying nursing tree gives life to the birthing seed. H.W

CHANGE

SETTING FOOT ALONG THE TRAIL

Since I was a child, I have had fun playing among the trees. Their fat, gnarled roots, spread out on top of the dirt, made imaginary rooms in my tree house on the ground. In the fall, I raked their leaves into walls that separated the rooms of my leaf house on the lawn. When I hiked among the trees and into the woods with my teenage friends, we would light a bonfire to roast hotdogs and burn marshmallows on thin sticks. When we camped in a clearing, listening to the sound of the gurgling creek or the roar of the rapids, trees outlined our campsite.

Now I am entering the forest on my spiritual journey, and I find that it takes courage to take that first step. I am afraid of the unknown. Will it be a jungle, with scary vines poised to trip me? Will it be a tropical forest, misty with heat and humidity? Will it be a sparsely treed forest near the desert, on hard, dry, red earth? Such questions cause some fearful anxiety as I make the decision to set foot along the trail.

Happily, what I find is the woodlands of my youth. From the stand of maple trees, the sap ran freely during the cold nights and warm days of spring and was the source of delicious maple syrup. In winter, two Clydesdale horses harnessed with collars of real jingle bells pulled the sleigh as we rode through that same stand of trees. Now that I am much older, the path is winding and flat, and it zigzags between and around the maple trees. Clumps of clay and knotty branches make the walking difficult.

Coming upon a forest river, I enter the cooling water. I am dragged under by the ancient, traditional, Christian baggage I am carrying with me. I am a good swimmer, and usually I can hold my head above water, but I am struggling. The thought forms: perhaps I should let go of some of my bags and *let the current carry me. Letting go does offer me new opportunities. I rest by floating on my back. I change to different strokes and swim the distance.*

The good news is that I have begun to go a little deeper. My base camp is Christianity; coming out of that heritage, I should find the spiritual trail base camp to be familiar territory.

At least, so goes my thinking.

COURAGE TO GROW

Change: The Neutral Zone

Change began for me in the last century. Back then, one of the frequently heard phrases was, 'Change is the only constant,' which Heraclitus originally said a few centuries B.C. Yes, I have lived the future shock of too much change too quickly. In the early 1960s and 70s, I talked about that change with my head; I knew it intellectually. Known, comfortable patterns of everyday living were ending. The women's liberation movement, the contraceptive pill, and a more permissive society ended many traditional ways of living. But so much so quickly: our society and its institutions were in the early stages of transition.

Old patterns died, but new ones had not yet been shaped. Sociologists invented the theory of transition to help us understand what was happening in society. In the model of transition, whenever there is an end, there is a neutral zone of waiting. It is a period of anticipation and frustration. In the last century, waiting for the new thing to come put society into states of disengagement, dissatisfaction, disenchantment, and disorganization (Bridges, 2004). I began to feel separated from my world, let down by everything and everybody around me. 'New' just didn't seem to work the way I expected it to, and nothing seemed to run as smoothly as before. In my head, I understood that these feelings of discomfort were not unusual; this wilderness neutral zone of change means living in constant turmoil. However, the model didn't tell me how my gut would feel. Change! I was to find out that it really is the only constant.

My husband and I had both retired, another one of those transition times. I did not work at my career job. There were grandchildren to enjoy. As a spiritual director, I had often said to the person with whom I was walking, "As your personal life goes, so goes your spiritual life." Therefore, I also recognized the changes in my spiritual practice. With more time spent in the quiet of our home, now an empty nest, I did not feel the need to get away so often on those 5-day silent retreats. I spent contemplative time in the house, in the forest, even in the public swimming pool. I enjoyed the practice of Yoga and its accompanying meditative poses. All of these changes are normal and healthy. All were part of my continual growing process, and as change keeps happening I keep moving in and out of the neutral zone. Connection and separation, familiar and strange, are hallmarks of transition, growth, and development.

Self-Development

When I walked in the forest, the softness of its floor felt gentle to my feet, and it occurred to me that I had not thought of the forest itself transitioning. But. Leaves fall. They decay. The dark decomposition changes into the fertile soil that creates a nourishing bed for the seeds to germinate and grow into the saplings of the next generation. Change must also be constant for the forest in order for it to become rejuvenated.

I continued into this century to live the shock of change. To have the courage to grow, at any age, for any reason, one must have the courage to change. When a tree grows, it changes its height. It grows taller. When a bud grows, it changes into a flower filled with colour. In my personal growth as a woman, I had changed also. Like a flower bud, I had moved through many images of myself:

- From maid and mother to homemaker (I began our marriage before the feminist revolution).

- From 'just a housewife' and 'wife of' to person, partner, parent, priest, and pastor (I enjoy the freedom of the women's lib movement as well as the love and respect of my husband and children).

- From parent to grandparent (Ross and I parented three children and have two grandchildren).

- Much of the credit for my living through these transitions has to go to my parents who gave me the assurance that it was OK to ask questions and encouraged me every step of the way. I can honestly say that the 'fear of the Lord' was never a signpost on the trail to change. I just slowly but surely "grew in wisdom and stature" and in the growing, change took place.

Faith Development

In the Church as an institution and in Christianity as its faith, there have been many changes. The first Protestant Reformation began in the 16th century when the priest Martin Luther nailed his complaints to the door of his parish church. Today we are living through the second Christian reformation, which began in the 1940s. It is acknowledged that the Christian era came to a halt during World War II. Change and its surrounding circumstances have brought us to a post-Christian era. For some, this religion is in transition from a formal construct created by men for mankind to an emerging spiritual worldview inclusive of all creation.

As I read the Gospels, the spiritual ferment raging at the time of Jesus sounded vaguely similar to the spiritual ferment raging in our time. The emerging spirituality of 1st century Galilee led to a new form of religion known to us today as Christianity, but it evolved out of Judaism. In the midst of today's spiritual awakenings, I wondered, is a new religion metamorphosing out of Christianity? As the spiritual ferment continued in religion, so it continued to ferment in my faith-life.

I remembered once again the imperative of the forest: decay and fermentation are necessary for its perpetual growth.

Similarly, in my faith-life growth, I had changed. My theological belief system changed. I moved through many images of God, Jesus, Holy Spirit, and the Bible, as well as the Church and its doctrines and creeds. The purpose of my story is to tell you about some of those changes, giving you a glimpse into one person's spiritual evolution. You may find that you have experienced many of the same changes, perhaps just not naming them in the same manner.

Around each bend in the trail, there were new experiences: cell groups, experimentation with different liturgies, silent retreats, and leadership development. For me, it was harmless enough, yet exciting; it was fearful enough, yet stimulating. The roots of faith were nourished to grow. A long time ago when I entered this spiritual forest, I read that faith was the opposite of fear. Now that was a hurdle to jump over and to assimilate on my journey! I read also that without doubt there can be no faith. This was reassuring. I followed the path to find that I had to climb over another large, decaying, fallen tree, but this time I realized that I did have the courage to grow.

My growth and hence the change were influenced by reading, discussions, study, re-evaluation of my beliefs and the church's doctrines, silence, reflection, and conversations with my spiritual director. How did the images and beliefs in my holy faith get re-formed? In chronological order, here is what happened in a nutshell:

- By joining a cell group in our congregation as a young woman in my 20s, (1960s), I took the first step of this long, slow spiritual journey. The cell was created on a similar principle to the cell in our body; it divides and starts a new cell. After spending a certain length of time as a group, we would separate and start new cell groups. However, this didn't happen. Our group of four couples, which met weekly, wanted to stay together. We were the first couple to leave the cell when we moved to another city. Our discussions in the cell group were about the books we had read. The most thought-provoking were by Paul Tillich The *New Being (1955)*, *The Courage To Be (1957)*, and *The Eternal Now (1963)* and John T. Robinson's blockbuster Ho*nest To God (1963)*. Both are now classics and I am most grateful for their contribution to my journey. During these discussions I stopped believing in a physical place for heaven and hell.

- By reading and discussing books whose contents were breaking new theological ground in the 1960s and '70s, I was always nurtured in my spiritual quest. God for me was re-shaped from a God above, a supreme being, omnipotent in all things, to God who is the ground of my being, a divine presence who dwells within my soul. I was amazed that nothing drastic happened to me when I ventured into new God territory. (Chicken Little might have cried 'the sky is falling the sky is falling,' but I was not affected.)

- By joining a house church with other families, some of them members of our congregation, others not part of any church, we developed our own style of being a gathered community. The adults met weekly for prayer and discussion. Once again the topics were current theological concepts. Once a month, our house church families had a meeting in which our children were included for an afternoon and evening of activity — seasonal crafts, movies, baseball games, swimming — after which we gathered for a potluck dinner, singing, and worship.

- By receiving encouragement from my husband and other members of my family to re-educate, in 1979, I entered a ten-year process to earn a Bachelor of Theology and a Master of Divinity. I made that decision on the weekend that Ross took our children on a camping trip and left me at home to ponder, to wait on the Spirit, to hear what God was saying to me. When they returned, I confirmed to Ross that I did want to answer God's call to become an ordained minister, thereby stepping out on a faith journey without knowing where it would take me.

- By discovering, through biblical and historical criticism that The Holy Bible was just a library of many shorter books written by men BCE (Before Current Era) and in the 1st century CE (Current Era), I changed my acceptance of biblical authority forever. The bible became a reference book for reflection on living rather than an authoritative rule enforced by the church.

- By re-evaluating the doctrines, dogmas, and creeds of the 4th and 5th centuries CE, I shifted my approach to these teachings. Documents of absolute authority within the hierarchical church system were no longer credible to me. Yet dynamic new statements of faith written by many Protestant denominations in various countries, like A Creed written in 1968 by the United Church of Canada, gave me hope for positive change both in the church and in my spiritual growth.

- By entering silent retreats (extended periods of silence broken only by conversations with my spiritual director), I took time to listen to God, the ground of my being dwelling within. Beginning in 1984, I continue to go on retreat two or three times a year. It is a nurturing time for me.

- By taking the training required to become an accredited spiritual director, I set off on a spiritual path that beckoned me into a ministry of spiritual companioning. I began to take this new evolution in my spiritual journey seriously by introducing new elements into my ministry to the business community: spiritual direction, silent retreats, faith-work luncheons, and discussions on ethics and business.

- These events helped re-shape and re-form my spiritual life.

I had walked into the forest and found an old cedar tree that had become the nursing tree for the new sapling growing out of its centre.

You may have noticed that this path wound in and through the avenues of the church but did not keep exclusively to the well-worn trails. And all the time the journey continued with others. I did not travel alone. The courage to grow, the time to change, came within the field of familial support and was enhanced by literary mentors and teachers from many walks of life, as well as new friends whom I had met along the way. Yes, I was enthused and eager to travel the theological highways and byways, seeking the emerging spiritual worldview. No, I was not surprised that I had had the courage to grow. The surprise is that I am now writing about my spiritual evolution!

Having the courage to grow was like stopping to look at the cocoon and watching as the butterfly struggled to come out and fly away.

First time meeting Jesus ca. 1944

This part of my story began with my first awareness of meeting Jesus as a little girl, six, perhaps seven years old. It happened on my walks home from a Brownie meeting. Our Brownie pack met after school, from 4:00 — 6:00 p.m., in the Scout Club House about five blocks from my home. Not a long walk, but in the wintertime it was a dark, cold, lonely walk. Each street corner had a streetlight and sometimes there would be one in the middle of the block. This is when Jesus was with me. He and I would walk together from one light post to the other. I knew he was with me because all the way home I would sing the hymn "Jesus loves me this I know," and I was not afraid of the dark night or the lonely cold. I marveled at the sparkling, pure, white snow dancing ahead of me. I skipped and sang my way home. Jesus continued to walk with me in the songs learned at Sunday School, songs like, "Breathe on me, breath of God," "What a friend we have in Jesus," and "Jesus us bids us shine." Here, then were my first images of Jesus — as my friend, my protector, and my encourager.

From My Journal

Metamorphosis

In the cocoon we live in the in-between-time.
Outside the cocoon institutions and organizations
in Health, Education, Religion, Politics.
Commerce, Family, Work,
are painfully shifting,
Traditions collapsing — metamorphosis.
Now the era is post-Christian, the church considered irrelevant.
Yet our souls search for nourishment.
Our hope is with us in the cocoon.
We emerge, flying.
Institutions re-shaped, re-named,
Organizations re-formed, re-membered
ca. 1988

There Is A Time

There is a time for everything
A time for every season under the sun;
A time to be empty
And a time to be full;
A time to be naïve
And a time to know;
A time to nourish
And a time to be nourished;
A time to doubt self
And a time to take self seriously;
A time to lead
And a time to be led;
A time to follow

And a time to lead;
A time to inspire
And a time to re-inspire;
A time to be blessed
And a time to bless;
A time to keep
And a time to throw away. July, 1996 (Reflections Ecclesiastes 3:1-8).

Holy One, I Hear You

'Harlene', I have called you by name, you are mine.
because you are precious in my sight,
and honoured, and I love you,
I will be with you.
Do not fear, for I am with you.
Do not remember former things,
or consider things of old.
I am about to do a new thing; now it springs forth.
Do you not perceive it?
Harlene, for you I will make a way
in the wilderness, rivers in the desert.
Come. Receive.
You are standing on the edge of the old,
ready to see new visions.
Come, and do not be afraid.
I hold you in the palm of my hand.'
"Yes God, I hear you. Amen. Jan. 1994
(Reflections Isaiah 43:1-5,18-19)

LEAVING THE WELL TRAMPED TRAIL

Having just walked through the maple woods, I follow my path down to a river. Although there is a gently moving current, the water is too deep and the stream too wide to wade across to the opposite side. But the river's sandy bottom is so inviting that I just walk in anyway and swim along with the current.

On other occasions, this religious stream has been kind to me — no physical abuse by priests, no sexual harassment, and no overt threats of control or fear of punishment from a paternalistic, omnipotent God. Once again I believe that the Christian current will support me. I have not been scraped by jagged rocks, nor pushed by strong currents. However, leaves swirling around me on the water and the now slightly turbulent current troubles my contentment.

Finally, I reach the other side and continue my spiritual quest; there is evidence that things might not be the same as they were in the maple woods. Here, the forest floor shows evidence of fallen branches, uprooted trees, and moss scraped off rocks. Gusts of wind come up from behind me; strong winds are a-blowin'.

LETTING GO

Change: Happens

For decades I had heard about the paradigm shift — a shift in the
pattern of living our values, a change in our religious beliefs. In a
gradual evolution of my personal understanding of God, Jesus, and
Spirit, I came to the *kairos* time, the opportune time, for me to
begin to live that paradigm shift. Kairos is the Greek word meaning
opportunity, the time when the conditions are right to take decisive
action. The more common Greek word for time is chronos, that time
measured by the clock or calendar. From the depth of my intuitive
knowing, the shift happened in my own sacred kairos time, not in
society's chronos time.

Like a fox caught in a leg hold trap, waiting for the conservation
officer to set her free, I waited for the paradigm shift to come to
the church.

I recalled the story about Katie Ford, a student in Bishop John
Shelby Spong's class at the Harvard School of Divinity, who wrote
a sermon on the Christian creeds. She stunned the class with her
unique perception. She said, "This creed has become for me an
unlivable place" (Spong, 2001, p.253). I agreed with her that the
creeds were unlivable. For example, in those creeds we repeat the
Trinitarian doctrine naming God as one deity and three persons —
the Father, the Son and the Holy Spirit. This doctrine blocked me
and hindered my progress on my spirit trail.

The Trinitarian doctrine was and still is regarded as the orthodox
or correct approach to Christianity. Since its inception in 325 C.E.,

it is repeated every time one says The Nicene Creed or The Apostles' Creed. Perhaps it was appropriate for the uneducated populace in the 4th and 5th centuries. Babes in their knowledge of Christianity, they were fed the symbols and memory work of the creeds in order for them to learn the teaching and beliefs created by the early church.

However, for me to make any change in my belief system meant that I had to let go; that meant letting go of the system of theologies that had been taught to me and that now entrapped me. This letting go was not an overnight phenomenon. From the early 1960's until the early 2000's, it happened in kairos time, not chronos time. Let me list the beliefs and practices from which I have slowly but surely moved away:

God who lives up there out there
The omnipotence of God
The naming of the deity as God the Father
The anthropomorphic God (attributing human form to god)
Jesus as one part of the Godhead
Spirit as one part of the Godhead
Jesus as God, fully divine
Jesus as Man, fully human
The physical resurrection of Jesus
Jesus as my personal saviour
The sinful nature of 'man'
A physical place called hell
A physical place called heaven
The historicity of the bible
The literalism of the bible
The absolute authority of the bible
The authority of the church
Worship of the Trinitarian God (Father, Son, Holy Spirit)
The Nicene Creed, the Apostles' Creed
Attendance at worship services

These doctrines and teachings confined my spirit. Church officers and Faith and Theology committees stuck in a quagmire of ancient history and beliefs were blocking my growth. I waited impatiently for the picture to change.

In my heart, I was grateful that I was able to name this letting go that felt comforting to my spiritual health. Experiencing my first conversion was like renovating my Christian faith. There was no vacuum: as each item fell away, there was simply space for the new. Perhaps this was the beginning of being able to speak my inner holy truth. My sense of ease gave me freedom from church-imposed labels of gnostic, subversive, or heretic. Because a sacred presence filled my whole inner self, because the very ground of my being was holy, sacred and good, I did not feel a loss.

The first big letting go was of the concepts of heaven and hell which, as I have mentioned, took place in our cell group. For all of my young life, I had worried that if I was a 'bad' girl, I would go to hell, that underground place of fire and damnation. On the other hand, if I was a good girl, I would go to heaven, that place of peace and life with the angels in the sky. However, letting go of the physical places of hell and heaven became an imperative. In this conversion, I adopted a different concept of heaven, one that spoke of being within the grace of God's love while living life on earth. Likewise, a place after death called hell became re-formed into a different concept of hell, of being alienated from God's love right here on earth.

Of course, no new idea is immediately grasped.

Second time meeting Jesus — once more 1980

From those childhood days of knowing Jesus as my friend and protector, I didn't meet Jesus — again for the first time — until I was a mother of three teenagers, wife of a busy corporate executive, church volunteer, and student in the Vancouver School of Theology. It happened in the first class of our New Testament course. The professor's opening remarks centred on those bibles that had every word that Jesus spoke printed in red. Many of us had grown up reading red-lettered bibles. We were shocked to hear him tell us that Jesus did not say one word that was printed in red ink. It was questionable if he said any of the words the Gospel writers had him saying. The professor continued that it isn't even a sure thing that Jesus was even born.

From writings outside the bible, it is known that someone called Christos was crucified.

Students left that class in tears, in anger, in frustration, in disbelief. For each of us, it was the beginning of a walk along a new religious / spiritual path, the beginning of a search for the answer to the question "Who do you say I am?," posed by Jesus, according to the writer of the Gospel According to Matthew. My first New Testament class initiated my second conversion and initiated a chain reaction that would continue for a lifetime. The professor's pedagogy worked. I have spent the last 35 years answering who Jesus was/ is/ will be?

In the intervening years, I have come to grips with some of my questions about who Jesus is for me. There was old baggage, tattered and torn — like the red-lettered bible — which I discarded. There was old luggage, tried and true — like favourite Christmas carols — which I could no longer carry with me. There were new backpacks, sturdy and comfortable — like understanding Jesus as my interpreter of God — that took me to new places along the path in my understanding of the Christian faith. But the actual releasing and letting go of my traditionally learned images of Jesus, God, and the Holy Spirit, the letting go of the doctrines and the creeds of the church, re-adjusting my beliefs about the authority of the bible, and really living that transformation — all this came slowly through decades of continuous searching. The trap had been sprung. I was free. Leaves were swirling above the water's current and falling off the trees in the new forest and I was wildly running through them.

The new waiting began, waiting for the powers–that–be in the church to shift forward. I am the tree. My leaves have dropped, my branches are bare. What comes next? Will the weather change, bringing breezes for new growth?

Effects on my Spiritual Life

After letting go of childhood images of God, the first thing I had to change was my prayer-life. When Jesus was my friend, then God was the authority figure. That old suitcase full of pictures of God up there, out there, the old man in the heavens, to whom I sent many prayers of request (and, of course, I was doing all the talking) was exchanged for a new briefcase. It is relatively easy to talk to God in prayer when naming and picturing God as the Father up there in heaven. Actually, in seminary we were taught that our prayers should include four sections: praise, thanksgiving, confession, and petition. However, since I now saw God as the indwelling ground of my being, a divine presence that is an invisible dimension of my reality, it was inevitable that praying would take different formats and different methods. Prayer became meditative and contemplative. The transformed adult, me, now sits quietly to reflect upon the situations in my life and the lives of those around me. I listen to the wisdom of the still small voice within, and then in faith I respond. Unwittingly, I was on my way to learning as the mystics learn.

Once again, this letting go of traditional ways of praying took years. It was probably ten years after the letting-go process that I recognized that contemplative prayer had become natural to me. I was having minor surgery. Just prior to going into the operating room, I began to pray in my evolving mode of prayer. Instead of speaking words to God and asking for whatever it was I thought I needed to get me through the ordeal of surgery, I simply sat in a chair, gowned, waiting for the nurse to fetch me, and prayed contemplatively. I was left alone for about thirty minutes, during which time I practiced the breathing exercises I had learned in yoga and kept my mind on the present with meditation. God, source of love, and ground of being engulfed me. I entered the OR relaxed, mentally and emotionally prepared. This very tangible prayer shift I count as my third conversion, welcoming me into the realm of mysticism and spirituality.

It was okay to let go of the God of my childhood. The mystery of how faith develops, the wisdom in ageing, and the practice of living in the present moment freed me to experience divine presence in quite an exceptional way. This meditative way of 'praying' — staying in the present — had given me the grace to be accompanied. From my heart and mind emanated the energy of the Holy Spirit, which I experienced as inner strength, and I felt confident that I would be guided through the surgery and on to recuperation.

I had walked into the strong current of the river and its flow had carried me safely downstream. I had grabbed onto a floating log and allowed its strong bark to hold me while the healing waters soothed and embraced me.

Through the years, during this metamorphosis of my prayer life, I had filled the briefcase with readings about the early mystics — Hildegard of Bingen, Julian of Norwich, and Meister Eckhart — as well as twentieth century mystics — Edward Hayes, Henri Nouwen, and John Gorsuch. Religious women of the 20th century — those whom we once called 'nuns' — women like Joyce Rupp, Joan Chittister and Mother Teresa became, via their writings, my spiritual mentors. These mystics told about their profound spiritual experiences. Fortunately, I was encouraged by my spiritual director to write of my own spiritual experiences. The poetry, psalms, free verse, and reflections which I wrote in my journal are the compositions I include at the end of each chapter.

Identifying with mystics and calling myself a mystic encouraged me to take myself seriously in shifting to a new way to practice my faith-life. From an authoritarian male deity when I was a child, to an all-encompassing circle of love, my images of the power of God have changed immeasurably. Now as an elder, I invoke various metaphors for imaging the holy: the ground of my being, the source of life, unconditional love, divine presence, ultimate reality, holy mystery, sacred wisdom.

From My Journal

Dianue

Spirit Divine you circle me.
And God says: Dianue (it is enough)
Spirit Divine you inspire me.
And God says: Dianue
Spirit Divine you accept me.
And God says: Dianue
Circle, Inspire, Accept
And I say: It is enough Dianue!
August 1995

The Gardener

I.
Holy vine grower,
you come to me
with loving hands
snipping away the
long stemmed, woody
old growth
preparing the way
for new growth
small leaves at vine's junction.
Holy vine grower
you choose
with loving hands
which leaves to keep
which to prune.
Holy vine grower
I am your vine

deep rooted
fertilized with your new spirit.
My roots soak
in the spirit of your love.
Holy vine grower
I am your vine my roots are deep enough
my stems are strong enough
prune me
that I will grow.
Sacred vine grower
how precious are all the vines
in your care.
II.
You sprinkle us with clean water;
you clear away the stones;
you set our tendrils in right places;
how wonderful are we in your care.
Sacred vine grower
oh one of green thumb,
let your secret ingredient
pour into our hearts,
we are immersed in your love.
III.
Creator God, your wind rustles by my body
and you are over me.
Source of all Life, your peace stirs my heart
and you are within me.
Ground of my Being, you prune and fertilize
and I am centred in you.
All in All.
Divine Presence
you carry, encourage, and care
and I rest in you.
You abide in me.
August, 1995.
(Reflections John 15:1- 4.)

LOOKING FOR NEW TRAILS

Ever careful, I keep my eyes down, watching for the tree stump or the root that might trip me, the stones that make the walking difficult. Up until now, I have carefully followed the true and narrow path of my theological training.

Having crossed the river safely, I am encouraged to cast my eyes in another direction. Having shed old baggage, I carry a light satchel-backpack. The maple hardwood stand of my childhood is far behind me. But in some of my childhood stories, forests might be magical places — like a woodland of cavorting leprechauns and fairies. Also, there are many fairy tales that induce fear, like Hansel and Gretel dropping bread crumbs or Little Red Riding Hood walking to her grandmother's house.

I walk on, following a path through low shrubs, past the bramble, and gaze at the vista ahead. As if by magic, the forest becomes an unknown land. Although this theological path will not be magical, it could be awe-inspiring. Here though, a grassy meadow welcomes me to a differing terrain: shades of mauve, white, and yellow alpine flowers form patches of colour in pastures of golden-green grass. Then I peer into the distance and glimpse the hard, black, igneous tusk left by the erosion of the mountain's volcano. It is jutting into the cloudless blue sky.

Wandering along, I see signs posting warnings about the trail ahead. "We accept no liability if you don't follow the rules" reads one. Further along, "Beware — new landslide," and, "Danger. Stay on the trail. Do not go out of bounds." Oh my, I think.

PARADIGM SHIFT

Change: Transformational

The religious paradigm shift that has occurred during the last 60 years was a transformation that many chose to ignore. In my Christian arena, our family would attend church on Sundays, and Ross and I would attend a study group mid-week where we at least talked about this shock of change. Although the group's identifying name changed — cell group in the 1960s, house church in the 1970s — basically the programme was the same. We read current, ground-breaking, ferment-causing books about the research and questions in which theologians were involved. Man made in the image of God? Why not woman made in the image of God too? Why not God both male and female? These revolutionary notions were the stuff of our discussions in the '60s and '70s. The locale of God, heaven and hell, not up there out there, but within each one of us, guided the changes in our language for understanding God. The way we referred to God changed from *thee / thou*, to *he/him*, or *she/her*, and gave us food for thought. We dropped the King James translation of the Holy Bible in preference for the many new versions that had hit the bookshelves. But within the hallowed halls of the sanctuary, it was the status quo.

By the beginning of the '80s, these now slightly subversive groups entered into the big theological questions. Our group developed our own style of worship which emerged from our current reading material and what we were learning. We started each meeting with a check-in, creating a caring community; we included a communal prayer; those who felt comfortable tried to use 'inclusive feminist language' (even that was a new term for us). We did not take up time planning the programme: it happened spontaneously from our need to know. Our energy for social justice was funneled into responding to the growing youth migration across Canada. We organized a drop-in centre in the church basement, and provided a 'crash pad' for them in our homes. New Christian songs with feminist language circulated among us at weekend retreats and workshops. In retrospect, we had begun living the new dichotomy.

On Sunday in church we sang, "Holy, holy, holy, lord God almighty .... cherubim and seraphim falling down before thee" (Heber, ca. 1820).

Gratefully, midweek in house church we sang songs written in the 1970s that were circulating orally. I was energized by this positive effervescence and our participation in it.

In the Land of "Don't Know"

In 1977, I made the decision to re-educate and to become an ordained minister within 'my' Church, the United Church of Canada. I felt that my particular call, or goal, was to speak this new theology to the business community in downtown Vancouver. At the Vancouver School of Theology, I chose courses that extended my new learning, the latest in academic theology and contemporary Christian spirituality.

With so many changes all around me, as I sauntered along my faith-life path one day, I was nudged to reflect on the process in which I had engaged. It could help me understand my own mid-life journey. I took a week off to spend time at a directed silent retreat. Reading and doing the suggested exercises, I delved into both my emotional and spiritual growth. The book *Dear Heart, Come Home: the Path of Midlife Spirituality*, by Joyce Rupp, had chapter titles like "Midlife Searching: Old Maps No Longer Work" and "Midlife Transformation: Shedding the Skin" (Rupp, 1990). Rupp asked questions, then invited readers to find the answer within themselves. I learned that I was on a journey where the old maps — support groups, lunches, Sunday church, and congregational work — no longer worked for me. Rupp referred to the words of the Korean Zen Master Seung Sahn, about "living in the land of don't know," (Rupp, 1990,p.65) and I immediately recognized myself. He wrote that to be in the land of 'don't know' was good because it freed wisdom to emerge. It was a place of waiting and trusting. Living in the land of 'don't know' was not a time of confusion where one kept reinventing the wheel trying to get out; rather, life in the land of 'don't know' was a time of openness, thinking and acting outside the box.

I was forty, in 1977, when I started my re-education. I had one motto: "I am a woman in the process of becoming." I was living in the land of 'don't know'. This was a healthy place from which to initiate a new type of Christian ministry aimed at the men and women in the business community of downtown Vancouver. This ministry provided a space for spiritual and ethical discussions. Borrowing from my own motto, I would say about Workplace Ministry, "It is a ministry in the process of becoming." In 2011, celebrating its 25th year under volunteer leadership, the ministry is called Workplace Centre for Ethics and Spirituality. It has been continually changing and is still becoming. I, too, have been continually changing, and I am still a woman in the process of becoming, a senior now, but still on the faith-life path. Both the ministry and I, living in the land of 'don't know,' were free to make room for newness of the Spirit and to shift out of the traditional system. I lived in that land of 'don't know' for many, many years. I have found that this is an essential part of the faith-life journey — confusion, frustration, going in and out of doubting, then re-opening into faith, letting go some more. There were fresh starts, each going deeper into my interior self. Gradually, I moved to a different kind of awareness, adapting into another conversion.

The paradigm shift, though it was talked about, was slow to take place in the church. Ironically the best models of change came from the nuns and priests in the Roman Catholic Church. These religious leaders, who were feeling the strain of an authoritative religion, embraced the ferment.

At the United Church Conference Centre in Naramata, B.C., I attended a five-day retreat on spirituality. The theme speaker Diarmuid O Murchu, a Roman Catholic priest from London, England, was making a North American tour discussing science and spirituality. Before starting his first lecture he made a disclaimer: what he had to say was entirely his own thinking and research; because his work was not accepted by the church, he was flying under the radar of the Vatican. In 2013, still a working priest researching and touring the world, he is famous and well within the radar's range. Perhaps the Vatican dare not excommunicate him because of his popularity and because what he has to say is correct.

My alma mater, VST, sponsored a weekend workshop that featured an American 'woman religious' in the Roman Catholic Church. Before she began, she asked that all recording devices be turned off. She said that she only had two years until retirement and that she didn't want to be asked to take an early leave. Although her book had been vetted by the Vatican, her lecture would be about the current unrest; she would not be talking about the book per se. The religious unsettlement continued during the 1990s.

Third time meeting Jesus — once more. 1985

The shift in knowing who Jesus was for me continued. I learned that stories about the life of Jesus differed. The four gospels told about his physical life from their perspectives. The letters that the apostle Paul wrote to the people in the emerging churches in Corinth, Thessalonica, Galatia, Philippi, Ephesus, and Rome said more about Jesus the Christ than about Jesus the man. I spent many hours trying to figure out who was the divine Jesus, who was the human Jesus, and what was the Christ.

There were a few things that I had sorted out: one cannot and should not write the life history of Jesus. The stories about Jesus in the Christian Testament and those about Moses in the Hebrew Testament each pointed to the relationship between God and humanity; Paul, in the New Testament, wrote about 'Christ within,' which is similar to 'the still small voice within' that we read about in the Old Testament. Both of the Testaments depicted humanity's search for spiritual truth. That was me, a woman in search of spiritual truth.

While in seminary, I read that icon-breaking book, *Jesus, An Experiment in Christology* (1979), by the Flemish Roman Catholic theologian Edward Schillebeeckx. It was an "experiment" because the church had not adopted his hypothesis. The book has a section called "Jesus, parable of God and paradigm of humanity" (Schillebeeckx, 1979, p.626). Schillebeeckx called Jesus the metaphor of God and the model of humanity. This appealed to me. In fact, I wrote my Christological paper on the book. It was Schillebeeckx's work that essentially re-shaped my Christological thinking. The phrase, 'parable of God, paradigm of humanity' inspired, energized and pushed me to adjust once more. From 1994 on, I began every sermon by repeating, "I speak to you in the name of Jesus of Nazareth, my Interpreter of God."

After reading and adopting Schillebeeckx's ideas, I converted from seeing Jesus as my personal friend to seeing him as a metaphor, from seeing him as the one I supposed to be a man in history to the one who, for me, was the model or the epitome of what it means to be human. I ventured forth again to find the elusive answer to the question about Jesus, "Who do you say that I am?"

Seminary education and biblical exploration took me to the Jesus Seminar scholars, who published their work on the search for the authentic words of Jesus as a part of their academic search for the historical Jesus. Their work, *The Five Gospels: The Search for the Authentic Words of Jesus,* (Funk 1993) determined that very few phrases or sentences attributed to Jesus were originally spoken by him. It can therefore be said that most of the Jesus sayings, anecdotes, and conversations in the Gospels were either created by the gospel writers, or they came from the oral tradition, or they were expressions frequently used in the Greco-Roman world of his time. It became apparent that my shifting perception of who Jesus was for me was affirmed at every bend in the road.

Difficult as it may be to believe, I kept searching for encouragement and wondered, "Do others think and feel as I do about Jesus and God?" So I posed this question to a former moderator of the United Church of Canada, The Very Reverend Robert Smith: "Is Jesus God?" Looking at me straight on and speaking gently but confidently, he replied, "That is not for me an appropriate question for the 21st century." Whew! What a relief that was to hear. In his caring and sensitivity for all of the members of the United Church of Canada and for the spectrum of our divergent views, he neither confirmed nor denied that Jesus was God, but directed me to ask the appropriate questions. My spiritual quest needed that declaration.

Nevertheless, his words dropped like kindling on the glowing embers of an unattended campfire and were left to burn. Tiny flames crept along roots underground and in time my forest erupted into flames. Branches burned. The charred remains of trees blackened a small swath of the mountainside. New theological seeds began germinating from the fire's debris. I remembered the warning signs in the grassy meadow.

After my reading of the work done by Schillebeeckx and the Jesus Seminar group, I have never again been able to believe that Jesus was God come to earth. When at Christmas we said, Jesus, Emmanuel, and God with us, I inevitably had to do an instantaneous, unconscious, theological update. My update went like this: The birth of Jesus reminds me that divine spirit is born and lives in the hearts of all people, and that is worthy of celebration. 'Is Jesus God?' — the question is only appropriate for the early Christians steeped in Greek mythology.

A Different Vocabulary for a Different Time

We, though, must ask new questions for this era. Living in the age of information, the population of the 21st century is well-informed, educated, and at liberty to think freely. Adults with overwhelming options needed to find a new vocabulary for the Christian lexicon — including me, if I was to be true to my call into the ministry. I searched for language to satisfy the
hunger created by my questions about contemporary values, beliefs and spirituality.

Of course all of this made sense to me; the former moderator was right. Certainly, my questions concerning the Holy would not be the same as those of people living in the 3rd, 4th & 5th centuries when our Christian doctrines of God, Jesus and Spirit were developed. I hoped that some day soon, the answers to my questions would actually speak to my understanding and experiences in the 20th and 21st centuries instead of coming from the early centuries. To paraphrase a popular parable from the Gospels of Mark, Matthew and Luke, 'You can't pour new wine into old wineskins.' While I was working as a professional clergywoman in the Church, I constantly tried to pour new wine into old wineskins, to speak a Christian spiritual language using contemporary words, but it became increasingly difficult to translate — to re-interpret.

During a silent retreat in 1996, I doodled my thoughts in my journal, once again with this traditional Father-Son-Holy Ghost Trinitarian notion of God. Journal entries remind me that I took a playful approach, reflecting on four forms of the holy. Instead of the Holy Trinity, I came up with the numinous quadra — God, Christ, Spirit, Self; Christians would have a quadrune doctrine of god. It was then that my Christian spirit trail ended and I hiked in yet another direction, from the limited triune God to a God of limitless dimensions. I chose the fir tree as my symbol of new presence. At that time, this holy image became a simile: God is like a tree. The trunk is Wisdom or Sophia; the roots are Christ; the branches are Self; the needles are Spirit; the cones are the fruit of the Spirit — love, joy, peace, patience, kindness, goodness, faithfulness, humility, self-control.

Still living in the land of 'don't know,' open to thinking outside the box, I ventured to push aside the Trinitarian blockade and wrote, "God is wisdom, love, and spirit, made known by Jesus the anointed one (the Christ) through the centre of self." My image of God had changed and another paradigm shift had occurred. My spirituality was being altered one conversion at a time.

The metaphorical image of this chapter, 'looking for new trails' encouraged me to carry only a light satchel. I shed the old baggage during this search for a new Christian paradigm. I wanted to find a language for this spirituality. I stopped using the traditional word

'God' and tried adopting its Greek counterpart, 'Theos.' This kind of thinking supported and undergirded my evolving faith. To shed the old baggage that the word God carries with it is to let go of a heavenly deity in the human form of a lord, a master, a father, or a king. Into my new satchel, I put the conceptualization of a sacred presence, the ground of my being, which I called variously spirit energy, unconditional love, and divine presence. Perhaps, I speculated, I can signal my evolving use of the word 'God' by introducing the Greek word 'Theos' into the lexicon. God is shown in the personhood of everyone; Theos is real when we celebrate the sacred presence in every person.

Or I could say that the core of this new spirituality is the dwelling place of divine presence; it is about the wisdom within each of us. When we are connected to that ground of our being, we experience joy and contentment — heaven on earth. When we are not connected to the ground of our being, we experience hell on earth. 'Sin' is another term that comes loaded with centuries of language inappropriate for the 21st century. However, in each of us there is the shadow side to our personality which, when it is not psychologically and emotionally balanced, can cause us to commit evil or do harm to ourselves or others. The notion and the words of 'original sin' and 'sinning' have been deleted from my database.

I re-named the act of prayer by practicing varying forms of meditation, contemplation, centreing, reading, thinking, feeling, and reflecting, and combining these with breathing exercises. I chose to refer to this time as my quiet-time. I created my own version of meditation and other forms of listening to the 'still small voice.' My prayer life continued its transformation within my new paradigm.

Beyond Belief Systems

During this personal time of spiritual unrest, my spiritual director said to me that she had a hunch that I had grown not only beyond the United Church of Canada, but also beyond Christian denominations by any name. One of her clues was the story I told her about attending a United Church Women's Conference in Banff, Alberta.

We were placed in small groups and asked to introduce ourselves by giving our name and home congregation. I astonished myself when I heard myself say, "I am Harlene Walker. I attend St. Andrew's Wesley church in Vancouver, but my spiritual home is Bethlehem Retreat Centre on Vancouver Island."

That was when I realized that home congregation was not about a building, or a religious home full of systems, teachings, hierarchy, tradition, and control. That description was of a religion with God on the outside. Home congregation was about a spirituality where I got in touch with the blessings of unconditional love and connected with holiness: the creator in nature, the sacredness of meditation, the theos of compassion, divine love, and source of life accompanied me when I served the community with grace and justice. Such action was spirituality with sacred presence within my soul.

It went further. Not only had I grown beyond the church as I knew it, but that day I grew beyond religion. Did I really want to? I was afraid to move outside my comfort zone, outside of a Christian community. I was afraid to move beyond belief. If I was beyond belief, then what was left?

I was grateful that my faith in the Jesus spirit kept me grounded. Richard Rohr, in his book *The Naked Now*, added the missing word for me — I had moved beyond belief *systems*. (Rohr, 2006, p.29) "Just keep breathing," I wrote in my journal. Meditative breathing, learned through Yoga practice, had eased spiritual transformation and moved me toward recognizing the transcendent presence in inner experiences. My faith was grounded in the Jesus narrative, not stuck in religion; I stood poised in the reality of a new faith dawning.

Purposefully, I headed in a new direction and made footprints towards that not-yet identified faith.

From My Journal

Universal Theos

Theos is a grand ocean
pulsating with the tides of many religions.
Receiving.
Faith is a mighty river
flowing with numerous spirit streams.
Receiving.
Christianity is one
trickling spirit stream.
Receiving.
ca. 1990

Trees

Like the trees in the fall that let go of their leaves,
I stand tall, my heart strong in the knowledge that
when I let go, new growth begins.
Like the trees in the spring that regenerate buds,
I stand tall; my heart-love pulls at summer's full growth.
Come Spirit Energy fill me with strength,
let your sun shine into my wisdom.
Guide me to calm,
freedom, release,
I continue the process.
Today: I stand firm in spirit energy, Presence of all calm.
Nov. 2012

Sacred Calm

Sacred One of All Calm
hear my heart's preoccupations.
I find calmness in you.
Holy One
I give to you my endless fretting
I find calmness in you.
Spirit Presence of All Calm
I release the ties that restrict my freedom
I need calmness to let go.
ca. 2010

Transformation

I saw the desert across which every soul must travel to reach the next stage of living, and the name of that desert was transition ....and I saw a truck which conveys souls across the desert, and the name of that truck was patience.

I saw the forest into which every soul must walk to reach the next stage of living, and the name of that forest was fear....and I saw the one who guides souls through the forest, and the name of that one was courage.

I saw the garden in which every soul must rest to reach the next stage of living, and the name of that garden was joy....and I saw the person who holds souls in that garden, and the name of that person was friend.

Nov. 2012

Personal Notes and Reflections

Answers grow out of the questions. H.W.

A NEW PARADIGM

WALKING IN THE INTERPRETIVE FOREST

The trailhead to Loggers' Lake begins by inviting the hiker to walk through the Interpretive Forest. At intervals along the path, information boxes are built. Some of the boxes have written descriptions and pictures of the flora and fauna growing in this particular mountain forest. I stand by a box, look at the tall evergreen tree directly in front of me, and read that it is a mountain hemlock. Under the tree, very small hemlock cones litter the ground. Pictures and the description of the slow-growing tree, its bark, its flat needles, and its tiny cones give a succinct interpretation of the real-life scene all around me. Boxes further on display details about good forest management. Inquisitive visitors new to the mountain area could have many of their questions answered just by taking a walk in the woods.

I too am an inquisitive visitor starting out on this metaphorical spiritual trail. At regular intervals, I find information boxes made up of books, work- shops, retreats, and inspirational leaders. Will this interpretive forest answer any of my questions? Do I know how to ask the appropriate questions for the 21st century? Am I really ready for profound change?

APPROPRIATE QUESTIONS FOR ME

Interpretation: Keeping On Track

This journey has taught me the importance of the appropriate question. Any social theme must be re-examined in the context of it's culture and era. Speaking generally about generational attitudes, my parents, born in the early 1900s, reached back to the Victorian era for their understanding of religion; I, one of the silent generation, reached forward into the Boomers' generation, living my own evolving experience of Christianity; our nephews, born as Boomers, have been seeking transformation and freedom in all areas of life — educational, societal, personal and religious; our children, however, growing up in the chaos and uncertainty of all that was changing in the 1960s have become pragmatic, realistic, anti-institutional and non-religious in their diversity.

We who were born into these generations have either accepted the traditional answers to questions laid down for us in past centuries, or we have walked away. When I think of religious questions and the answers found in papal bulls, articles of faith, catechisms, and the midrash, exacting words pop into my mind: definite, absolute, and acclaimed as 'the truth.'

Ushering in a new century and the second millennium, our grand-children, called the millennial generation, are considered the most loved, optimistic, and hopeful of all the generations in the last one hundred years, but they are the least interested in religion; however, they are open to spirituality, open to a variety of ideas, and able to connect more easily with anyone, regardless of colour, culture, language, or other differences. I am impressed by the way they are integrating these positive attributes into their work and lifestyle.

It is, I believe, the Millennials who will teach us how to ask the questions and, as importantly, how to find the answers for this era. When I listen to the interviews of many of the founders of big tech companies, most of whom are in their 20s, I hear stories of innovation, brainstorming, cooperation, and partnership. They ask a question, then do research and develop the answer into a product. They do not come up with absolute answers. Indeed this to them is an impediment to open-ended thinking. They also know that what is developed will either be of no value, commercially viable, merged into a bigger group, or re-shaped by another innovator. And for them that is okay. I'm guessing that Henry Ford, of another generation, would not be so flexible.

Being advised to seek appropriate questions for this century and to let go of questions and answers from another millennium, I continued to search for affirmation that I was on the right track to a vision of spirituality I could offer to my grandchildren. I stopped in front of one of the information boxes in this forest and spent some time listening to the questions now swirling around in my mind.

Who are my mentors?

I was born with a pioneering spirit; I curiously wandered along the trails of spirituality in search of mentors and personal truth. Many who do not have this inheritance would not dare to walk the journey.

My personal mentors have been my parents, my husband, my spiritual directors (who happened to be Benedictine Sisters), and my soul friends, who showed me values, suggested detours, offered helpful hints, and continuously fed me with nurturing soul food.

Of all of the hundreds of authors whose books and articles have fallen on to the path, perhaps I could pick half a dozen as having influenced me the most. My literary mentors have been the Church of England Bishop John T. Robinson, German theologian Paul Tillich, Flemmish theologian Edward Schillebeeckx, Benedictine Sister Joan Chittister, Joyce Rupp of the Servants of Mary, and

Diarmuid O'Murchu of the Sacred Heart Missionaries, England. They are spiritual innovators who acted as models and mobilizers; their writings gave me the freedom to grow into my potential as a mature and balanced human being. Mentors, theologians, spiritual directors, and soul friends in Europe, Canada, and the United States have influenced my spirituality and evolving Christian faith-life. I was not alone.

The Canadian elder journalist Peter C. Newman enlightened me with his distinction between a paradigm *shift* and a paradigm *change*. His statement, "Change demands inspired leadership. Shift happens" (Newman, 2004, 26), gave me cause to look at my transformation from another perspective. Over the years, a paradigm *shift* was taking place outwardly: shifting to using inclusive language, rationalizing doctrines, renewing the liturgy, revitalizing the congregation, welcoming nontraditional ministries. My understanding of faith, of the system of religious beliefs, was shifting on the outside.

Simultaneously, within me, the paradigm *change* was taking place: in how I pray, in my concept of deity, in my worship, and in my understanding of spirituality. My very humanness was changing on the inside. This distinction between a paradigm shift and a paradigm change helped me to acknowledge that each of my mentors was an inspirational leader who led me to the paradigm *change* that I live today. Without noting this difference, I could not have had this insight: sustained inspirational leadership motivated the profound conversions taking place within my spirituality. This spiritual evolution was not cosmetic.

Am I in a time of confusion or conversion?

As a pilgrim on a spiritual journey, after reading about the land of 'don't know,' I knew that I had traveled in that land. It was a good and encouraging place to be. I re-read some of my journal entries from 1983. They tracked my travels:

"I had to pray with ( ) tonight. I didn't stop to analyze to whom I was speaking—I had to talk to somebody. My God and the power of God's spirit were with us in the bedroom." (01/05/83)

"I need from you understanding, trust, acceptance, love. You need from me understanding, trust, respect, acceptance, love. "We both receive from Jesus love, acceptance, respect, understanding, trust. In his stories we find the person who can fulfill these fine basic human needs." (08/05/83)

"We can't see wind. We can't see heat. We can't see love. We can't see power. We can't see God. We feel wind, heat, love, power. We feel God—but why do we worship God?" (08/05/83)

"Faith is to believe in God". (06/09/83)

"To know about the healing power of the Holy Spirit is to be able to let go of all the inner doubts and rotten gut feelings.

The love of God we feel from others. It can overcome the fear that we feel inside. Our inner 'wolves' need to be freed, faced head on. " (07/09/83)

"I see God as a being who isn't powerful enough to change what I want to change, but who is caring enough to be with me in what I'm about.". (05/10/83)

When I read these entries twenty years later, they look like a measuring stick from ground zero. I have walked a long, long, way on the path to conversion.

What are my core strengths? What is my truth?

In '85, my language didn't include words like 'core strength':

"I believe that Christianity is one vehicle that carries me on a journey to experience the spiritual dimension of my human nature". (25/01/85)

However, fast forward twenty-two years and my core strength was deeper:

"I listened to Gary's audio sermon about Jesus coming to his disciples Peter, James, John, fishing from their boats, but their nets are empty. (Luke 5:4-11) Gary called this a story about Jesus popping up in front of anyone at anytime, getting in the boat and saying, 'Nets empty? Go deeper!' Here is a metaphor: Spirit Energy accompanies us and encourages us to go deeper. When *the* story connected with *my (our)* story, I realized that my coping, adjusting, and working through various mental disorders that were present within my family, gave me some skill, faith, and commitment to go a little deeper. I had walked and talked with them through the deep waters; L

Love, sacred presence, had always been my anchor. I looked for support from all members of the family and community; I reached out for help; I talked with my Spiritual Director, my soul mates, and a psychologist.

May the Energy of Holy Power sustain and guide in the days to come. Let me go deep—with Jesus-like friends in the boat with me. As in the past I have to speak my truth." (24/02/07)

"The voice in my soul cried out.

The voice in my soul cried–

The voice in my soul–

The voice–." (24/04/2010)

My core strength began to emerge in the public arena. I was frequently asked to say the grace or an invocation at public functions: Board of Trade, Rotary, Vancouver City Police Department, conferences. Integrating traditional language with my new lexicon when speaking, I tried to be faithful to this interior strength.

Saying Grace at Christmas to a Rotary Club:

"This is the time when we remember our sacred story: in the Jewish faith through Hanukkah, in the Christian faith through the birth of a child. Each is a story of God present in our lives. Let us pray.

Holy One in the hush of this place we breathe in the calm of *your* life (silence) in the silence we breathe out the busyness of *our* life. (silence)

We come seeking your love, hope, peace, joy.

Gift us with your lively compassion and justice.

Glory to you O God on Earth peace goodwill to all. Amen"

A Benediction:

"May the invisible power of wisdom rest upon our hearts.

May the invisible power of our intuition, the invisible power of the strength of our faith, and the guidance of Wisdom lead us."

Personal Mantras:

"Compassionate Presence hold me in your Love."

"Peace, peace, peace, Om!"

In the interpretive forest, I met my authentic self, and I liked the person I met. This land encouraged my wisdom to percolate through the soil of my heart, flavouring my thoughts with ideas that spilled outside the institutional spiritual box.

During this time of transformation and conversion, my awareness of my own identity had changed. Yes I am 'Doc' Hind's daughter, Ross Walker's wife, Geordie, Sandy and Cam's mom, but I am also Harlene, my own separate self. I have lived through the women's liberation movement and freed myself from stereotypical female roles. I have lived four of Shakespeare's seven stages of life. Now, as an elder, I am at the fifth stage, the age of the crone, and I am harvesting my lifetime of experiences. I embraced a new model of spirituality and spoke the truth of my authentic self.

Finding my truth was in part a journey through the experience of a 5-day intrapersonal lab and then making use of personality templates like the Myers-Briggs Indicator and the Enneagram. Making sense and connecting the dots came from the continual input by my spiritual director. At one point when I was in retirement, I met with her and told her that my intention was to listen to the spirit and to hear what my call would be for the next few years. She suggested that I continue my work in spiritual direction, that my wisdom, experience and heart have provided the qualities to be a good spiritual director, and that I should stay in the practice. "Don't worry about more education or academics, your inner wisdom is sufficient. In our Benedictine language, you are a stable person," she said. She also recommended another session of the Enneagram approach to knowing self, which I did.

It had been about ten years since I had been typed by an Enneagram resource person. This time I saw my traits in a different light and I heard the teacher differently. Sister Jill, my spiritual director, had given me good advice. I am a #7 in the Enneagram typology; the warning wakeup call for us 7's is that 'the grass is always greener on the other side.' I will always need to be aware of being pulled in every direction; #7's, it suggested, stay focused and don't get distracted or scattered. Staying in the present, concentrating, will give me the most productivity and gratification. Boredom, another warning sign, is my anxiety when the environment is not providing adequate stimulation. I do not want to be tied down; anytime I'm feeling bored, I must stop to see what I am avoiding. (Reflecting on this Enneagram information, I realized that lately my boredom had been from avoiding making the decision about what to do with my life in retirement.) Taken to the extreme, my dark side is the cycle of anticipation-craving-excess-escapism-addiction.

On the other hand, on my light side, I have many strengths upon which to build. I can generate ideas quickly and spontaneously, look at the big picture, initiate, and commit to my vision. (Advice to me: don't ignore negative feelings; recognize my impatience and its root cause; take time to bring my abilities to fruition.) The willingness to explore, well-rounded knowledge, multi-tasking, and versatility with a positive attitude, offered me great flexibility in retirement. Grounded, steady and stable, spiritual direction and pastoral care were still workable alternatives for me.

I also learned that the commandment to love your neighbour as you love yourself is best demonstrated by first loving yourself, which then releases energy to love your neighbour. I express the values of love, kindness, gentleness, joy, goodness, acceptance, compassion, loyalty, integrity, self-control, trustfulness, and patience from the perspective of an extrovert.

The effect of this learning about my spiritual evolution was to help me integrate the wholeness of a quiet, focused mind with an active physical purpose. In my journal I wrote, "Fulfillment comes from letting go of getting; letting go allows the riches of the present moment to touch me, which leads to experiencing the deep abiding pleasures of life, like every fall day hearing the pinecones fall on the roof at 7:20 in the morning. I can see the spiritual in the material world and the divine in the ordinary abundant life."

Finally, there were other tools that helped me to know my truth, like visualization and dialogue writing. I would write a wisdom-letter to sacred presence, something I always found very helpful for listening to my inner small voice. One time, I had visualized the sacred as a rose bush. The dialogue after that visualization was written when

I was not entirely confident in using the new lexicon; I wrote it addressed to God.

Harlene: Thank you God, divine presence in my life, you have come to me via the Enneagram and the New Testament.

God: How else would you know me but via the Word and my people?

H. I am relieved to acknowledge my personality type, too many eggs in one basket. I accept myself as that woman.

G. At last! Take that sabbatical I am always with you. You are grounded in my roots and will continue to grow from my trunk.

H. Here once again you come to me in the image of a tree. A rose bush. Where is the cross?

G. The cross is made from a tree. You carry it with you all of the time. Why not wear the one you have as a reminder of whose you are?

I will continue to grow in my own self knowledge (November 2002).

Entering more deeply into the struggles that life put in my way, I continued to keep in mind that my journey inward beckoned me but did not take me away from the stress of daily living. On the contrary, with my spiritual life renewed and energized, I was able to step into the fray in my home, in my profession, and in my community. The call continued.

APPROPRIATE QUESTIONS FOR TODAY

Interpretation:

What does 21ˢᵗ century spirituality begin to look like?

This century's spirituality, if I can be a mystical forecaster, could take on the image of wisdom and compassion rather than buildings, worship, doctrine and dogma. Those who wish to move deeper into the qualities of their inner being will be encouraged to attend to their core wisdom. Accompanied by a trained spiritual companion who, like a mid-wife, may walk with them, they will be helped to give birth to the essence of their interior spirit. Contemporary spirituality will be wise, compassionate, and full of goodness.

I had walked along the trail in the interpretive forest and read the information printed in the boxes, which had stimulated my contemporary questions. Now I became the information box, stimulating our friends' curiosity about our contemporary non-church, yet, faith lifestyle. Our friends asked, "What will you and Ross do if you don't 'go to church'?" I didn't answer in any detail, but I am sure that we probably did what past generations have done. We chose the best from our experiences, expanded that, created new experiences, and began to live all over again. I became aware that when the traditional sacred rituals have lost their meaning, men and women create their own more significant responses to the sacred. For us, the ordinary becomes the sacred.

Since Ross and I were empty-nesters and were not running off to attend church any more, Sunday became the day for us to re-connect. We planned at least one activity together. Having 'Sunday dinner' was re-visited; we decided to invite one or two friends who might be alone that evening to join us for dinner and watch TV together or have a game of cards.

Personally, I continued to recognize the Sabbath, only not on a Sunday, and I designed it differently with a time set aside from regular weekly activities. Usually every 8-10 days, I designated one day as a quiet day. From breakfast to dinner, I would spend the time in silence; I would walk, read, and reflect. It was not worship or church, but it was my Sabbath. Weekend silent retreats remained a constant source of spiritual nurture. I maintained membership in the professional organization called Spiritual Directors International which kept me in touch with my vocation. Its magazine, *Presence: An International Journal of Spiritual Direction*, became my main resource for personal spiritual development; it updated me on the current literature and connected me to the global cultural context.

What are my new maps?

Once upon a retreat time, while doing my Yoga practice and listening to music, the words from Joyce Rupp's poem, "Stars in my Heart" (1996, p.3) surfaced in my thoughts. After exercising, I knelt on my prayer stool, moved into the silence of meditative prayer, and began to ponder the 'stars in my heart.' Just as the stars bring light to the black night sky, so stars in my heart had become a metaphor for bringing sparkle and brightness into my inner self. Out of lived experience, stars in my heart helped me to identify new rituals and 'maps' that would guide me to re-imagined spirituality.

The most important map was music. There always has been music in my life; I had now identified its importance. Music permeated my life: sitting beside my mother on the piano bench while she played her beloved music, singing in choirs, quietly chanting, attending concerts, listening to symphonic music, dancing — music matched my mood.

During the 1980s the chants from Taize, France travelled to this continent, souvenirs from those who had worshipped and sung with the community there. Taize music had become a new form of communication and spiritual nourishment among Christians around the world , Catholic, Protestant, young, old. Ecumenical theology, tuneful chants, easy to learn, it enriched the silence and enhanced meditation. Taize tapes and CDs were always in my silent retreat resource briefcase. To this day, music remains an essential map on this inward journey.

The designated place in our home for my quiet-time also became one of the maps on the road to 21st century spirituality. I added universal symbols to the centre piece. A Buddhist chime and a prayer scroll; a family photo; three olive wood figurines of a male, a female, and a child; an olive wood egg; the empty cross; and a figurine of a tree were the icons that created my meditation centre.

And, always, I felt the sacred presence of the ground of all being. I have never felt abandoned. From my journal:

God in my metaphor of Tree, God of Creation
God in my family and friends, God of Humanity
God in my everywhere, God of the Universe
God not of stagnant shrines, God of continuous creating
From Sacred Presence I do not walk away.
Come Trail-God, Liberate!Likewise, silence, walking, journaling, laughter, became significant in taking on the role of mapping my new spiritual practices.

In my metaphorical interpretive forest, to keep the trail clean, there are predator-proof garbage cans. At the beginning of this quest, I felt like the hiker using the garbage can to dispose of the unten-able, unlivable doctrines and teachings. Soon I felt like the predator turning the garbage can upside down. Bear-like, I looked for the still-good parts of the church; I wanted to scrape the bottom of the can, hoping to pick out morsels of healthy rituals and sacred symbols. Finally, unable to break open the garbage can, like the bear, I gave up the struggle and carried on. I had converted from religion to spirituality.

How do you teach (map) the sacred without a religious building?

Nature became a teacher. Sunsets have always had a special place in my heart. I love to sit and watch the sun setting on the water. The sun, vivid orange-red ball, changes shape and becomes that delicious-looking loaf of bread; how quickly it sinks into the water until sunrise. I love to linger, to spend the last few minutes in the stillness of the afterglow. In the summertime, we have spent holidays with our grandchildren. For the whole family, watching the sunset in front of the cottage used to be our habit. It was, if you will, a nightly spiritual ritual. After the sun had disappeared into the water, the children would join in singing an old camp song from my youth: "Day is done, gone the sun, from the lake, from the hills, from the sky, All is well, safely rest, God is nigh." It was one of those sacred moments when we would give love, hugs and kisses all around. Children have an innate understanding of the sacred which is up to us adults to nurture.

Hospitality and gratitude became teaching maps: children and adults too, have mentioned the something special about our home. Something as simple as saying grace: when we sat around the table to eat our meal, we joined hands and offered our gratitude for food, family, and friends. Thus, saying grace became a sacred ritual, a ritual that our adult children have passed down to their families. Walking the talk, for us, is all about living the sacred as an everyday-any-occasion-day opportunity for teaching about the sacred.

Integrating the participation of family members into the creation of rituals for the dying became a strong teaching tool: For many, the custom of asking a clergy person to officiate at a funeral or memorial service has changed. Christians who have left the church are creating their own conventions to recognize death and dying. It is known that terminally ill patients have a need and desire to gather together with their family, friends and colleagues. Putting closure to life, and offering a time of saying goodbye are occasions that can be celebrated before death occurs rather than later in memoriam. The dying husband of one of our friends requested a 'roast,' to which he invited his friends and family. The hospital chaplain cooperated, and four days later the man died. The family chose not to have any other type of memoriam. These days, I am asked to help families plan 'A Celebration of Life' for the one who has passed or to plan a roast as described. It is the family who plans and participates, making their memorial remembrances individual. I am their resource. These new spiritual rituals are tangible examples of the paradigm shift. The ritual is important. Since we live in the in-between time, many exiled Christians, non-believers and millennials have found viable substitutes for the orthodox funeral service.

What is a Spiritual Director Map?

A spiritual director is a trained companion. Like a map ,he or she acts as a guide who can walk with you on the spiritual path to a deeper understanding of holy mystery By listening to your questions, your story, and by talking with you, you will begin noticing in what places, and at what times sacred presence is in your life.

What is Spiritual Evolution?

When I was in seminary in the early 1980s I went into the office of the Professor of Spiritual Development and told him I would like to attend the silent retreat he was planning, and by the way did he have any books for me to read about God?" Our conversation went like this:
"Will this be your first time on a silent retreat?"
"Yes."
"Do you want to go deeper?"
"I don't know what you mean by that question."
"Well I won't give you any books to read about God, but come to the retreat."
And so began the practices that held my spirit as it evolved. Spiritual evolution is the growing familiarity of the many sacred experiences that came to me, opportunities that helped me to 'go deeper.' Both as a spiritual directee (one taking the retreat) and, later

as a spiritual director (one facilitating the retreat), I was drawn into the core of my being, listening to, and aware of, sacred presence in my life.

Unexpectedly, in my struggle with who God is for me, who Jesus is for me, and what Christian symbols are important to me, I have found out who I am. Throughout, there was this mantra: "I have always felt divine presence; I have never felt abandoned." This spiritual evolution has affected me both internally and externally. On the outside, physically my appearance has changed, notwithstanding the wrinkles etc. I do not make my hair curly with permanent chemicals, yet I keep it looking fresh and modern; I do not wear much jewelry, yet my attire is up to date; I do not wear much makeup, just basic skin care. On the inside, going deeper for me is about being true to myself, finding self, allowing for a natural transformation. This inward journey has led me toward individuation. I have learned to accept my privileged circumstances. I have had the good fortune to be physically and emotionally fit and well cared for economically. I have moved to simpler care of our home and of myself.

My spiritual community altered. In my journal drawings depicting this new kind of life, I drew roots, just roots growing in the soil. Unintentionally, I have gradually shown the spiritual root bigger and stronger. It is entwined around the community root, with tendrils encircling the family root, and all the roots are growing deep into the soil. Fifty-seven years old at the time that was how I pictured spiritual evolution: roots going deeper. My faith-life and my community and family life continued developing and growing deeper as my spirituality evolved.

Here is another way of answering the question about spiritual evolution: it is the change in the dialogue between the outer-me, Me, and the interior-me, Self.

Me: How open am I to going deeper?

Self: Remember when you asked Elly about books for the paper on God and he asked you if you wanted to go deeper?

Me: Yes. Today I do know what it means to go deeper and yes I want to go deeper. What do I need to continue my inner journey?

Self: Nothing more than you've needed before. You have been on a continuously deepening journey....You're just naming it now.

Me: Am I afraid of anything?

Self: No

Me: Is there something that I need to be attentive to?

Self: Yes. Focus on the moment, not events, stay in the present, not the future.

Such have been some of the maps that have led me through the interpretive forest of my evolving spirituality. I am accepting who I am and what I have to offer in spiritual leadership.

What is Universal Love for the Second Millennium?

Reflecting on this question led me to confirm that I have and do experience universal love through the experience of receiving my husband's unconditional love; I just never recognized it as a form of spirituality. Although I do have a *definition* of universal love, which I confess comes from antiquity. From the first century of the first millennium, when the New Testament was written, it is Paul's letter to the church in Corinth:

Love is patient and kind; love is not jealous or boastful; it is not arrogant or rude. Love does not insist on its own way; it is not irritable or resentful; it does not rejoice at wrong but rejoices in the right. Love bears all things, believes all things, hopes all things, endures all things. Love never ends. (I Corinthians 13:4-8)

This definition is one that I would read at almost every wedding ceremony.

Also, I have a *role model* of universal love. Jesus is my example. He is the parable of divine presence and a paradigm for humanity. If there is any body of work spoken by Jesus, scholars tell us it could be the stories that he told his small band of followers. The wisdom of the parables contains grains of universal love and demonstrates a universal loving lifestyle. The titles that have been attached to the parables bespeak a love that is universal and unconditional. Look for the spiritual truth in these stories: the lost coin, the lost sheep, the Good Samaritan, the mustard seed, the wedding guests, the wedding feast, and dozens more. One does not need to have a teacher to instruct us on the wisdom of love, truth and meaning found in any of the Gospels' similes, metaphors or, narratives; one can read, reflect, respond.

The disciples of Jesus began by receiving love from him, and then they and the little band of followers moved to defining him, love, and God, as they understood it in the context of the first century. We also can define it in the context of the 21st century. Such unconditional love is universal; I believe all who have a harmless, healthy, positive understanding of the divine are capable of the experience.

The questions continue but without absolute answers. How will a new spirituality be shaped? What will the new spirituality look like? Will people of differing spiritualities sit in harmony? Will spirituality develop its own doctrine and dogma, thus limiting spontaneity and varying practices? What obstacles stand in my way to compassionate living? The nourishing answers for each of us are to be found in personal research and development.

Personal Notes and Reflections

From My Journal

Nature's Icons

Meditate with the wind rushing
Concentrate
Meditate with the rain dancing
Concentrate
Meditate with the bird chirping
Contemplate nature's icons
                    July, 1992

Love of God in Jesus Love of God in my heart

Like a star in my heart
love twinkles humour and wisdom,
love blinks creativity and music,
love sparkles health and appreciation.
love of God in Jesus,
love of God in all humanity.
like a star in our darkness
love brings light to the depressed,
love offers healing to the confused,
love gives compassion to the hurt.
Love of God in Jesus
love of God in creation.
Like a star in our universe
no thing separates
no power overcomes
no being subdues.
Love, like a star in my heart,
shines continuously.
July 1996 (Reflections on Romans, 8:38, 39, and Rupp's "Star in My Heart")

Playful Spirituality

Music is the lifeline to my sacred self ~ sacred manna for my living.
Dancing ignites passionate laughter, romance, touch ~
nurturing body;
listening offers quiet enjoyment, connection, calmness ~
feeding mind;
singing calls forth joy, tears, companionship ~
nourishing spirit.
Music is my expression of spirituality ~strengthening body, mind
and soul.
    Jan. 2013
Music is manna for my soul
but I cannot live on bread alone.
silence speaks
wisdom intuits
sacred space offers solitude
circle of soul-mates strengthen
family holds the fragile whole
Such are the expressions of spirituality
for body, mind, and soul.
                        March 2013

Personal Notes and Reflections

Butterfly-like, faith and spirituality transform in the chrysalis,
and emerge in a new order as heart-wisdom. H.W.

CONVERSION

ENTERING THE OLD GROWTH TRAIL

Refreshed after the rest at the quiet place against the boulder, I wander over to one of my favourite trails into the Emerald Forest and its growth of centuries-old trees. I look up, way up, to see the forest canopy higher than a ten-storey building, where sunbeams, twirling through the lacy boughs, dance all the way down to the ground. I listen to the wind rustling the leaves in rhythm to the giant poplars' waving branches. Along the way, I particularly notice the trees felled by strong winds. Once straight, strong and tall, they now lie on the forest floor, transformed into nursing trees. Out of the decaying wood grow woodland flowers, dark green mosses, and tiny saplings, home to hundreds of insects; the dead tree nurtures new growth.

Finally, the upward trek curves along the abandoned loggers' road, and there it is ~ the first inspiring sight of one of the last stands of ancient cedars. I walk past once-majestic trees, their trunks now hollow, and the pecked bark shows holes created by pileated woodpeckers, squirrels, and burrowing animals. My attention intensifies; I examine the grove of old growth. Their trunks weakened by the decay at the centres, rock in the breezes, creaking and groaning above me. Like these ancient trees, I think, archaic sacred symbols are also in decay. I wander around in circles in a treed wilderness of decay.

TWENTY-FIVE YEARS IN THE WILDERNESS

The Legacy

Walking into the forest of old growth was awesome. The trees were at least one hundred feet tall and more than 100 years old. I knelt beside them on the thick, soft, emerald green moss. Their time was nearly over; every year they lived, they were at risk of being destroyed; it was not safe for them or for the hikers or the animals that passed underneath. An endangered species, very few clumps of these majestic trees would be left standing; they would be destroyed by strong winds, or cut down by the developers' backhoe. I, too, knew that my time of wandering in my wilderness of forests and streams must come to an end. Kairos time had once again struck its bell; soon ... maybe... perhaps ... I would be walking out of the land of 'don't know'.

Michener's novel *The Source A Novel* is a chronology of the evolution of the faith of the people who lived about 10,000 BCE in the land now known as Galilee. The characters had an intense desire to name and picture the mystery of their sacred living. From their yearning, they created the first clay images of their male gods, "for in those infinitely distant ages gods had not yet been called forth by the hunger of men" (Michener, 1965, pg. 69). That phrase held my attention and ignited my own imagination. My body tingled, and again I felt the stirring of questions. Is that what this spiritual yearning is about? Do I hunger to call forth the spirit of the ground of my being? Why is my restless spirit pacing up and down, back and forth?

A sharp tingling crept into my spiritual consciousness, calling forth yet another new spirituality.

I had to stop, to sit beside the old growth tree, and do some serious investigative, reflective reading.

I re-read O'Murchu's book *Reclaiming Spirituality: A New Spiritual Framework for Today's World,* (1998). As my understanding developed, I came up with this synoptic explanation. Before there was religion, there was spirituality.

Archeologists have found evidence of ritual burials from 70,000 years ago. For thousands of millennia, nomadic humans responded intuitively to a spiritual consciousness in their search for meaning and purpose to life. Then, what was probably one of the earliest paradigm shifts in the history of humanity took place about 8000 BCE. Known popularly as the Agricultural Revolution, it lasted until 1600 CE when the Industrial Revolution began. With the domestication of plants and animals came a shift in human consciousness. There was a desire to control the land and subdue the animals. Plans were introduced to grow more food, produce more animals, and have more fertile women. Concurrent with the development of this agenda there was a sense that pleasing the gods had something to do with increased abundance.

The next stages in the evolution of religions were the formalization of rituals and practices to please the gods, and the systemization of beliefs about the gods. Finally, with the manufacturing of clay statues imitating male and female humans, humankind had created its first symbols of male and female gods. Here I noted that *man* created gods in his image, rather than the Genesis version: God creating *man* in God's *own* image.... To the symbol was attached the concept of the sacred, and since each symbol was created by men it reflected the world-view of men. This was the birth of an idea called religion.

In the middle of the first agricultural revolution, around 5000 B.C.E., Hinduism evolved as the first formal religion. Only 2000 C.E. years ago, the world witnessed the unfolding of Christianity. At the time when religions were created, man's understanding of his world was limited to the information that came from his mind rather than from gathered factual or scientific data. In the prevailing patriarchal society, only males were acknowledged as human. Their wisdom dictated that the universe belonged to man to subdue and to dominate. Depending on the society, religious worship was addressed either to several gods (as in the polytheistic Hindu), or to one god (as in the monotheistic Jewish, Christian, and the Moslem). Each religion claimed divine revelation. With the rise of male power and its attending hierarchy, violent competition erupted among the religions, each declaring the supremacy of its religious truth.

Discrepancies in the legacy kept jumping out at me. Like the sacred clay images of men and women, the Christian holy scriptures emerged within a culture and tradition of the ancient Near East thousands of years ago. The early Greeks' understanding of a many-tiered universe influenced the Judeo-Christian image of gods; in heaven, gods were dominant, full of power and glory. Gods lived above the angels, and then, in descending order of importance came the sun, moon and stars; men, women and animals were at the bottom of the ladder. Satan lived in hell down under the world where he dominated, full of evil and damnation. Those archaic creeds came to us from the era of Plato's Greek worldview. Three thousand years ago men called forth one god and made that one god male. Such sacred symbols based on the culture, tradition, religion, and astronomy of past millennia had no meaning for me.

My wandering spirit hungered to call forth a spirituality based on the contemporary worldview of Hawking's universe (2011). The spiritual stirring that was happening to me and others like me was, I believed, a call for new rituals. This awakening invited twenty-first century men and women to rediscover the sacredness of an ancient spirituality within the context of our current social media and multi-layered cosmological universes.

Scientific Chaos and Shattered Symbols

The transformation of ideas, I reasoned, striving to emerge within 21st century Christianity, was like the transformation in the organization of subatomic particles and particles in the theory of chaos. The quantum physics theory of chaos embraces "unpredictability, discontinuity, and untidiness" (Hawking, 2011, pp. 63, 239). It gives the appearance of being out of control. Eventually, however, the atoms' particles whirling at random, in utter confusion, spontaneously re-organize and re-order themselves. Out of pandemonium comes a completely new order. The cosmos becomes an orderly system once again. Understandably, in the new order the atoms' behaviour becomes unrecognizable — so different, so changed that the old order becomes irrelevant!

It felt that for most of my spiritual journey I had been resisting the archaic patriarchal system, but no, the light bulb clicked on. I felt this frustration because I lived in a faith that was in chaos. It was the chaos within Christianity that was the source of my agitation. This insight was another wake-up call; the scientific theory of chaos was a helpful model as I struggled to understand theological disorder. Cosmologically, after the chaos comes a new order. This was for me a workable theory; I applied it to my spiritual frustration. After the confusion, there is a different arrangement. For example, in my changing faith-life, the tradition of Sunday worship needed to be shattered. According to the theory of chaos, the present old order will not be reassembled. It is simply redundant and no longer important.

I turned once again to the natural world for a metaphor in this spiritual paradigm shift. Mother Nature offered her cycle of birth, death, and re-birth. The decaying and dead trees of the old growth forest decompose into nutrients that give life to a new creation. Like the nursing tree of the ancient cedars, four-hundred-year-old articles of faith, three-hundred-year-old prayers, and centuries-old hymns (the ancient sacred symbols) deconstruct to become building blocks for fresh spiritual formations.

Taking time to read, to listen, to meditate, and then to write gave me the reassurance and the energy required to get up and start hiking the trail again. And lying there all that time on the ground beside me I noticed an old dead skin shed by a snake. I had just shed another layer of my religious skin.

In some forests, the indigenous people bend and tie saplings to point toward an important cave or source of water. The trees grow in that direction and become an Indian symbol tree. Religious symbols, like the Indian trees, point beyond, to the source of spirituality among us. Talking about the essential core of spiritual formation, making the transition from the classical meaning of symbols to new meaning with new symbols, was unsettling. I hasten to add that when sacred symbols are shattered, the belief they represented is crushed as well. This paradigm change profoundly touched me at an intense level of my consciousness. My heart and soul were moved. My faith-life had been completely upset. Within the chaos, the chalice, the cross, the bread, the wine, the host, the holy bible, the baptismal font, Jesus the Christ, and the church ~ all that I listed in 'letting go' at the beginning of this story ~ were well and truly unlivable places, symbols that no longer pointed to meaningful beliefs.

Fourth time meeting Jesus ~ once more, ca. 2005

When I met Jesus as my pattern for life and interpreter of God, the one whose path I wanted to follow, I was inspired. And yet....and yet in the back of my mind would be those niggling questions:

"Why are there miracles?"

"Why is there the virgin birth in only two gospels?"

"Why is Jesus walking through walls?"

"Why is so much of what happened to Jesus pre-told in the Old Testament?"

In my theological studies, six years were spent in formal education literally asking questions in classes, searching for answers from professors, finding literature in the school's library. I gained heart by repeating the phrase, 'without doubt there can be no faith.' Since I had doubt, I had faith. Doubt is the bridge I walked across to get to faith. Crossing that bridge led me onto the spiritual path. Rationalization and answers took root for me when I created my own metaphor for the Wesleyan Quadrilateral template for studying theological doctrine.

I drew a picture that looked like the inside of a four room house. Each room had a door opening into a common hall. According to the quadrilateral, each room had a name: experience, reason, scripture and tradition. The hallway was the passage to the Christian Trinity:

God the Father, the Son and the Holy Spirit. Anyone at anytime and in any order might spend time in one room and stay for as long as necessary to meet this God.

During the feminist movement in the '80s I lived in the room of tradition, moving from the classic model of women who were sidelined in religion to the contemporary models struggling to take shape, and onto the experimental models such as house church and cell groups. While at VST I attended classes in Denominational Studies, and at various times lived in all the rooms. In the room of scripture I studied courses in biblical Criticism and biblical historical Criticism, using many commentaries on the books in the bible, the creeds and systematic theology. Then I moved into the room of reason; out of that stay came the saying 'to believe, one does not have to leave your brain at the church door.' I was glad I could drop superstition and authoritarian concepts of the church. Finally, the room of experience welcomed me and I settled in. Those new spiritual roots began growing: silent retreats, music, meditation, contemplation, discussions, quiet times, listening, and attentiveness each had something important to say to me.

The four rooms were like a nursing tree for me; I began to see the possibilities for a new creation. Actually, my faith was now grounded in the biblical belief of the possibility of a new creation.

Many years later, in 2004, came another book whose author spoke to me. *The Pagan Christ the Lost Light* (2004) was written by Tom Harper, New Testament Professor at the University of Toronto. He introduced me to the allegorical Jesus, "the supreme dramatic symbol of divinity within us all" (Harper, p.180). Jesus was a symbol of sacred holiness within each person. Shattered symbols had been replaced by re-thinking Jesus, re-thinking allegory. With a reclaimed, fresh new meaning, my image of Jesus had shifted. It had been twenty years since I had met Jesus, not as a divine/human man but as a parable of God and paradigm of humanity. Treated as an historical figure, Jesus, who lived as any ordinary man, had become a model of divinity and a model for humanity. However, I had not considered that Jesus might not exist. With this new revelation, I saw that if treated as an allegory, like the Indian symbol tree that pointed to the source of water, the Jesus narrative pointed to the source of divinity present within each human, and the stories about him expounded a moral or spiritual truth.

Just as the contributions of others had encouraged me at various places along the spiritual path, Harper's contribution calmed my restless spirit. With care and understanding, he wrote about finding his answer to the question, "Who do you say that I am?" supposedly posed by Jesus in the gospel. *The Pagan Christ* invited me to review the origin of my faith and to revisit, again, my answer to that same question. It re-ignited my inspiration. From Harper's exposition of the Cosmic Christ based on ancient truths and myths, a new vision beckoned me in my ever-changing faith-life journey.

Wandering in wilderness time had been fundamental to me.

From My Journal

Words Words Words...No Word

In the beginning your Name was too scared to be pronounced, from generation unto generation the Name was given, like a hand-me-down of what was precious and sacred.

During each millennium people authored new meanings to your Name, out of antiquity into contemporary, Name speaks according to the era.

Neither stagnant nor inert, it moves, from beyond into our midst, from exterior to interior, giving meaning to all who seek.

In the beginning:
I am that I am. Yahweh.
First Century:
God, Father, Son, Holy Spirit,
Teacher, Shepherd, Eagle, Potter.
Twenty-First Century:
Sacred Presence, Unconditional Love,
Creator, Ground of Being, Ultimate Reality, Higher Power, Deep Well, Fountain of Wisdom, Absolute Mystery, Holy Mystery, Centre, etc., etc.
Today:
Names, for each day, three hundred and sixty-five names and more, have become a multitude of words.
I choose:
ground of my being, spirit-wisdom within,
holy mystery.
How choose you?
Jan. 2013

the stillpoint — still emerging

In the beginning humans were spiritual
rooted in an unknown spirit;
soon spirit became known
and named god.
To tell their stories men created gods
they called the study of the gods mythology;
soon men decided on one god
they called the study of God theology.
Civilizations created religion
sustained by theologian-built churches;
soon the spiritual was imprisoned
entombed in almighty cathedrals.
In the end-time of religion
soon seekers of the spiritual
found deep-faith in the spirit
nurtured as it was in the beginning-
outside of the cathedral.
Grounded in faith
not stuck in religion
soon societies were without religion;
now humans rooted in spirituality
live in a religion-less society.
Spirit unleashed, emerging.
June, 2013.

Divine Patience

Come patience of mine may your calm
be a balm to my life, my husband, my family.
Come patience of mine
pour your wisdom upon me.
Breathe in, calm — breathe out, smile -
let go, unwind — place of calm –
I embrace the road ahead.
Come spirit energy fill me with strength
let your sun shine into my inner wisdom.
Guide me to calm, freedom release.
I continue the journey ahead.

June, 2012

FINDING HOLY GROUND

The wilderness is vast, and I wander around for longer than I anticipated. Returning to my cathedral forest, I find that the master designer is redecorating. The spring, summer, and fall colours have changed. The new colours are dark emerald green, deep brown, black, grey, and white; winter is coming and the terrain is not quite the same as when I left it. Too bad I didn't bring my snowshoes. It is so much easier to make tracks in the snow, climb the gently sloping mountainside and clamber over the snow-covered fallen trees with a ski pole and snowshoes. In an evergreen forest of Douglas firs, hemlocks and cedars, the branches of the live trees are never bare. Their green needles and foliage filter the summer sun, but this winter canopy is not so brilliant; the sun is lower in the sky now.

It is peaceful here; there is a sense of holiness, a gift that nature often hands to me. Be still, shhh, listen to no sound — no calling birds, no whooshing wind, no animals brushing branches or crunching leaves, yet in that most silent of silences, I can faintly hear the gurgling flow of the mountain stream. I make a mental note to follow it later when it is frozen and perhaps take a photo of the waterfall sculptured in ice. Tramping in the forest through the four seasons, I marvel at what creation extends to us. Her beauty and its changing format show the intensity of her colours in the flora, fauna, and animals, confirming the origin of sacredness in all natural life.

NAMING HOLY GROUND

Sacred Places in Ordinary and Extraordinary Space

My spiritual paradigm was changing; it was happening. The winter terrain of the cathedral not only looked different but I began to feel its inspiration waning. Changing my spiritual paradigm from a single deity to an insightful wisdom pushed me into assuming responsibility for the fundamental aspects of living. The destruction of classic religious symbols is more than the absence of dogma and doctrine. It opens the heart. It brings freedom to respond to wisdom and patience, to listen for compassion. Each of us has that deep inner well of wisdom that I sense as spirit-wisdom. I don't pray to that wisdom, but I gain strength, courage and sage information from its energy within me. My steadfastness comes from the well of core perceptions, but I always need time to listen. To complete the paradigm change, an inspired leadership seemed to be emerging within.

Therefore, intuitively, I was pulled to explaining how I recognize the spiritual in my life. Where do I find it? And how do I feel it?

The Sacredness of the Ordinary At Home

Having a special place in our home designated as my sacred space has been a priority for me. This space has been in the kitchen beside the hot air register or in the living room in a comfortable chair, or kneeling on my prayer stool in the bedroom. I could also create a sacred space simply by placing icons on a window sill. While our children were in their growing years, a spiritual presence might engulf me in the living room while I sat listening to sacred music. The kids would look in at me and say, "Oh Mom is listening to her music." Respecting my privacy or not wanting to listen to the music, they would leave the room.

Over the years various ordinary items of special significance to me have become my sacred symbols and icons. In my mind each points to a spiritual theme:

a bouquet of flowers or a basket of plants > creation,

olive wood figurines of a man, a woman and a child in meditative positions > wisdom,

a cross with people painted on it, an egg made of olive wood > new life,

a Buddhist prayer wheel, a prayer gong, an eagle feather > spiritual universality,

a prayer stool > interior listening

a tree sculpture > holiness,

a family photo > values.

At this sacred centre, I meditate, practice Yoga, listen, read, reflect and journal.

Sacredness in Swimming

It was always fun to tell friends that I was going to Bethlehem for my silent retreat. This was true, sort of; the Benedictine Sisters had a monastery and retreat house in Nanaimo, B.C. They called it Bethlehem Retreat Centre. It became, as I have mentioned, my spiritual home; Ross would often go with me on retreat. Sister took a shine to him and we would often go home with a good bottle of her monastery wine. Any time of year was a good time to be there; seven acres of wooded trails, and a 45-minute jog around the lake provided ample opportunity for exercise or quiet conversation.

On a self-directed, five-day, silent retreat, as I was swimming by myself on a hot, July afternoon, I experienced what I have come to call the sacred in an ordinary place. I wrote.

Swimming today was wonderful–warm, calm, and again that feeling of peace that comes to me in these waters. I felt a presence of sacredness. Floating on my back, not moving arms or legs, just breathing to keep my head afloat and flowing with the current, I 'felt' the water gently form a circle around my chin, face and head and I immediately said to myself 'that feels like a halo. I am holy.' Then I heard, 'you are my beloved daughter in whom I am well pleased.' I began to tread water and spent much time pondering the experience that had just happened (July, 1996).

This paraphrase, 'beloved daughter,' from my gospel heritage, declared me a human being. From a psychological Jungian approach, it was my Self affirming my Ego. From my new paradigm, it was my inner spirit-wisdom affirming my outer personality. My development as an individual was transforming; it was essential for the evolution of both my faith and my spirituality.

The Sacredness of a Happening at the Seashore

Again my journal reminded me that on one of my retreats the spiritual director referred to my writing as inspired. The new and different surroundings of this particular retreat centre had become holy ground for me. To my surprise, she asked me to read 'Standing on My Stone of Struggle' at morning worship the next day. Instead of the biblical Epistle reading, I was to read an epistle of my own creation. The title was "Harlene's Epistle to those who have ears to hear":

'Standing on My Stone-of-Struggle'

"It is a sham to sing, 'Peace is flowing like a river.' Peace is not flowing like a river. It is a sham to sing, 'We are one in the Spirit.' We are not one; we are many in one Spirit. I ask myself, why do we even want to be as one?

Look at nature. The Pine trees growing on the bank, at the seashore's edge, are nurtured with fresh rainwater. The seaweed growing in the shallow ocean water, at the seashore's edge, is nurtured with salt water. Their roots grow, twisting, intertwining together, and in the same soil. The knarred tree roots, worn smooth by centuries of winds and waves, carve patterns on the earth's bluff. The long, slim, gelatinous hose of the seaweed undulates on the shore and in the water. Roots are not one; they are many growing together in harmony. I pick up a pinecone in the salt water. Camouflaged, other green-brown cones rest on top of the graveled seashelled beach. Stones, shells, cones, all are remnants removed from their source for the next generation of nature's resources. Harmonious. Not one. An *aha* spills over me. Food for my soul comes from the harmony in this diversity. My Spirit, Nature's Spirit, and Holy Spirit: this Holy Trinity is nourishment for my soul.

Pondering my question, I venture to walk this common ground wading further into the ocean's water where I try to stand on a rough-edged, water-flattened stone. Barnacled, little more than my two feet wide, with waves pushing back and forth, it is hard to keep still and I am surrounded by water. Slippery, it is a struggle to maintain my perch, but I am held, anchored only by my sense of balance. So I name it my stone-of-struggle.

The struggle continues amid the contentment. Where, I ask standing on my stone–of-struggle, do I recognize Jesus? Who do I say he is?

Jesus of Nazareth: first born? No

Jesus the Christ: anointed blessed one? Yes.

Jesus the Man: child of God? No.

Jesus: child of Love? Yes

You show me

abundant life

new way to life

the struggle in life.

Jesus you are Pattern for Life. (end of the Epistle)

I need to begin to speak with honesty; I need to preach my stone-of-struggle. All week I've tried to find a spiritual holiness near my cabin in the shade of the trees, the whispering of the grasses, and in the sunshine of the field. I have stayed away from the slippery rocky shore, the strange, hard uncomfortable shell beach so foreign to me. But today a still small voice spoke to me in that uncomfortable place while standing on my stone-of-struggle. While reflecting on creation-centred theology, I was engaged. And I heard, Jesus is Pattern for Life"

(July, 1992).

Sacred Places in Extraordinary Space

If beauty is in the eye of the beholder, then holiness is in the heart of the receiver. My husband did not usually whistle or burst into spontaneous song, except when he was skiing. There was no greater joy for him than cruising in fresh powder and singing all the way down the mountain. His favourite ski run was to him, what my forest cathedral was to me, a sanctuary.

Sanctuaries long acknowledged as the dwelling places of God, great buildings constructed to be the House of God, have been erected over the eons and around the world. Mosques, cathedrals, churches and temples beckon the faithful to enter. However, while visiting Italy one summer, a sacred presence overwhelmed me in one of the most unexpected of places. I certainly thought that the great *domas,* the cathedrals of marble, home of sculptures and paintings created by some of the greatest artists in history, would be places of spiritual renewal for me. But no, although I could admire the artistic workmanship, I did not respond as others have to their inspirational value. I became attuned to experiencing sacred presence in unusual places.

The Surprisingly Sacred Place in a Tower

One day while we were driving in the Tuscan countryside, Ross was drawn to a hilltop town away in the distance, and all that we could see was a fortress tower. We drove to the hill, climbed the rock steps and arrived at the castle of Rocca Di Tentennano. We entered the castle fortress and, joining other tourists on a regular tour, began our ascent of the tower. After the tour I took some time to be by myself, after reflection this is how I described in my journal, the entire extraordinary occasion.

"This tower differed from other towers. It had been restored with a modern perspective. Each room was bright with fluorescent lights; the stairway was a winding steel staircase suspended by cable. In the rooms, contemporary statues of today's men and women decorated the space. Up and up we went, room after room, four floors up to the top; we entered the brightest, most open, most spectacular area of it all. The whitewashed walls glowed with paintings of the same woman, head and face only, but in varying poses. The background in each of the paintings was a royal blue colour which enhanced her long silver hair and fair skin. I kept saying, "What a surprise, an art gallery at the top of a tower." Three or four rooms of paintings of this flowing, beautiful, peaceful young woman captured my soul.

My breath was stilled! Why?

My feelings of inspiration on seeing that woman quickened with excitement in my heart, a joy that I needed to share with Ross, our daughter and her friend. I ran out onto the ramparts of the tower to tell them about this current of energy. They felt nothing. For me, something different was pulsating in that castle's upper room. It was a familiar feeling, one I get when something deep inside moves and I respond to a sacred moment. Like an icon, the paintings of the woman initiated a connection with Holy Spirit.

On our descent, I finally started to read some of the inscriptions on the brass plates attached to the walls. What was this place? As we climbed up the tower, I had missed this piece of its history. On one plaque came important information: Catherine of Siena learned to read and write in this building. She lived in the region of Siena and this castle was her family's summer home.

With the support of UNESCO, the small towns in the surrounding area restored the fortress to honour her ministries among the poor and her work with the powerful men of her day. The paintings of the woman in the top rooms depicted the Holy Spirit, and the tower was a monument to an extraordinarily religious woman. A calm spiritual place of peace that honoured a woman!" (2005).

Saint Catherine of Siena (1347-1380) chose to be a nun. She was one of the female mystics I had read about. She was one rare woman: a feisty religious leader and a brilliant writer, philosopher and theologian who influenced both Popes and political leaders of her time. Six centuries after her birth, in 1970, the Roman Catholic Church would bestow upon her the title of Doctor of the Church.

It was there that sacred presence shone around me. Even hanging the paintings on the top floor, in the upper room of the castle signaled to Christians that this was sacred space, since the 'Upper Room' is so symbolic: it is the room where the disciples had their 'Last Supper.' Again I wrote in my journal:

The spirit overwhelmed me truly; I had just experienced an emotional depth of holiness in an unexpected place in Italy. Not in the sanctuary paintings, nor its carved marble, nor its ornate cathedrals but the Mystery of the Unexpected spoke to me in the distant hard rock hill of Rocca Di Tentennano (2005).

A sacred spirituality can be experienced at any time through the beholder's sensitivity to emotions.

Interior Sacred Space

When men believed in calling on God, they wrote in biblical language, 'the word of the Lord came to me,' or 'I have had a dream and in it God said.' The prophet Ezekiel saw visions: a wheel within a wheel whirling way in the middle of the air, or a valley filled with dry bones. The young man Joseph was called by Pharaoh to interpret his dream. John heard voices like trumpets and wrote what he saw in visions: seven lighted torches. Dreams and visions are universal, revelatory, and timeless.

In the present day, dream language is more likely to be understood in terms of Jungian psychology. From our deep subconscious, dreams bring messages to us. Dreams continue to be the indicator for me that a shift is about to occur within my spiritual experience, spiritual practice, or spiritual reflection; or that a shift has taken place and that I am not acknowledging the change. Dreams give me a 'heads up'; they are a 'be prepared' sign. However, that is not to say that the movement will happen immediately. It is always in kairos time, not chronos time. Always it is an opportune happening, not a timely tic-toc tic-toc event.

Sacred Place of Dreams

Water Dreams

Over the years while on this journey I have had repeated dreams with water themes and house themes.

Although the following spiritual dreams focused on water, the situation and locus was always different. In the dream, I was never worried about dying, although there were dreams that frightened me. Consequently, I looked forward to 'downloading' them for reflection and interpretation. What is interesting to me in retrospect is that when I first recognized these dreams and connected them to my spiritual growth, I noticed that in my earliest dreams the water was shallow; as I grew and as my faith deepened, the water in my dreams was deeper.

The water is tunneling around in an underground cave. I follow it, but I don't get lost.

My interpretation: trust God's leading, or, to update the language into my current experience of god and self: the ground of my being, source of life, carries me through my pain and my joy (1992).

A dream image captured a metaphor for me these days — body surfing. I feel as though I am riding the waves, a surge of energy takes me to the top, everything is going well and then the wave breaks (Nov. 1993).

Water dreams of danger and survival: turbulent water, silent deep water, slippery rocks, narrow passages high above the ocean and foaming waves below crashing against the sea's rocky cliff, I interpreted as signs of change. I was not worried — just alerted. As in the middle of winter when snow falls quietly, plants are dormant, and animals hibernate, dreams come in the most silent of silences while we, like nature, lie in the body's rest-filled sleep.

House Dreams

The last six months my dreams have been me in houses, big houses in which only a small section is lived. A big wing of the house is empty, sometimes it is furnished, other times it is not, but no one lives in it. The last house had seven bedrooms; my mother lived in one, and used one as her sunroom and I had one room.

My dreams have had me captive. The nightmarish house dreams have locked rooms or padded rooms. I can't get out. I remember one had a tiny cat door; the cat was bigger than I and he could make himself small to go through the door, but inside he towered over me, not hurting me. I just wanted out.

My interpretation: I named the house my body, my intellect, my potential, and I am only using part of my abilities. Or am I to stop what I am doing and begin something else. I thought that the cat dream was Workplace Ministry trapping me in work.

In response to these dreams I have stopped working 5 days. I take Fridays off. We have hired an Ordinand who is interested in an 'ethics ministry' and I am trying not to get overly involved in the programming.

"What am I called to do next?" (ca. 1993).

Many years later, in 2005, our son died, my mother died, and Ross and I decided to stop attending church—all within that one year. At the time, I didn't connect my dreaming with grief or with the personal changes in my life. However, the house dream returned. Although it was not frightening, it was 'interesting.'

Tonight I had another of my house dreams. A different house; the basement was finished into three big rooms groups of people wanted to have a seminar in the house. I thought that they could use the upstairs bedroom—unfinished and unfurnished. But when they arrived I took them downstairs to the three rooms; one had a kitchenette, it was perfect for snacks and as a breakaway room (2006).

This was different from my earlier house dreams. In those dreams, the big unused section of the house was always upstairs, always shut off from people and even I had to sneak in, take a peek and then rush out, closing the doors behind me.

My interpretation: The closed compartment was my secret desire to shift and to admit dis-ease with my spiritual life—worship, church and community. The new dream tells me to be open to my spirit life, not to live it in secret, to invite people into my new experiences of sacred presence.

In March of 2006, I visited my soul friend and, knowing that she would have an understanding of dreams, I told her about my latest house dreams. I was on the right wavelength; she helped me with this much fuller interpretation. After our conversation, I journaled.

"After the deaths, of my mother and son I begin to move through grief and start to engage with life again.

This is my spiritual house, and I am alone.

The upstairs is closed off to both me and my friends and visitors. I said "come to my house but don't go upstairs; I don't want you to know that it has an empty place." I take them downstairs.

The same closed-off-upstairs-dream recurred but with a difference. I invite people into my spiritual home and take them downstairs to the recreation area. Everyone mingles, enjoys the occasion, I serve food from the kitchenette, eat and talk in the breakout rooms off the rec room.

My grieving is still going on; I have lost my church community as well. For the third time I had this same dream—and again: I take friends into the red room for food and conversation. After the break I begin to tell people about my spiritual hunger for more than either the worship service or the institutional church was able to give.

My heart was now congruent with my mind. For years the first nightmare dream in the big empty house mirrored the in- congruency of what my heart's desire was, and what my mind's reasoning offered. I was living an incongruent spiritual life. I was living in a spiritual house full of furniture, the liturgical pews and the house were closed. That part of the house was empty, cold, unheated; there was no warmth emanating from its rooms; there was not any gesture of welcome.

The second dream mirrored the spiritual transformation that I was experiencing. There was warmth in the recreation room, furniture and sustenance welcomed everyone and the folk in the dream got to know each other. They stayed. They wanted to hear the story of my new faith congruency." (March 2006)

Sacred Space within Visualization

Moving inward, going deeper, ground of being, indwelling, interior core of wisdom these are all words that I use interchangeably when I refer to the sanctity and energy of my spirit-wisdom. For me this is language that is appropriate for 21st century discussions about holiness. I have a strong sense of such inner presence during guided visualizing, as well as in my dreams. Taking time to be quiet is one way to discern my holy ground. Sometimes I go through the process of discernment, or talk with one of my soul friends, or Spiritual Director, who can help with the interpretation of what I had dreamed or visualized.

"At a one-day seminar, the session ended with the leader guiding us in a visualization meditation. We were a group of about 10 people sitting on chairs in a circle. With our eyes closed and using our minds, we were directed to find a quiet place, to go to any place that was a favourite spot out of doors.

I went to my forest and sat down in the sunshine beaming through the trees. But all of a sudden I jumped from being in a beam of light in the cedar trees to sitting in the middle of an English country garden. All of the flowers were in bloom with beautiful colours; it was cool and I was surrounded by snow and beautiful mountains.

When the guided visualization was over we were asked to write what we had visualized. I did."

Later, at a different time when I had the next appointment with my Spiritual Director, I used this particular visualization to start off our discussion. She said moving from the old scene–cedar trees–to the new scene–country garden–was an affirmation of my personal blooming of who I am as a whole person.

In the slowness of kairos time, a year or so later, I wrote in my Journal.

"I have noticed that my contacts lately have been with people with new age thinking and with people from other religions. I picked up a copy of the *Shared Vision* magazine and I knew four of the contributing writers. So it came to me that perhaps my call has shifted. I started this ministry wanting to be a bridge between the business community and the church. Now I feel pulled to be a bridge between the new age spirituality and the church" (March 1996).

Sacred Place of Listening

I offer an example of how the core sense of spirituality emerges for me when I read, reflect, and respond and of how my inner spirit speaks to me via letter writing.

In 1997, I was on a three-day, self-directed, silent retreat at a Catholic retreat centre in Vancouver. As a resource, and for reflection, I was reading both *Opening the Windows of Wisdom* by Pope John XXIII (1996) and *Paul's Letter to the Romans.*

"Do not conform yourselves to the standards of the world.... be transformed inwardly....renewing your minds....discern what is good, acceptable and perfect" (Rom.12:2).

To do this, I used a specific tool I call 'read, reflect, respond':

Read: the book and the texts, then choose phrases that jump out at me.

Reflect: spend time thinking about their meaning and what the message is for me.

Respond: this time I wrote a letter to Spirit/Wisdom from Self. I asked questions and wrote affirmations or other statements that had come to me during the reflection time.

Self: all these years I have conformed to the church's public way of worship, and I have sought spiritual nourishment outside of the traditional Sunday service. Through retreats, Spiritual Direction, my personal spiritual discipline I have heard you speak in the depths of my being. Contemporary authors, composers, musicians, rituals, shape me. I am transformed, my mind/spirit renewed—not by dogma or doctrine but by scriptural wisdom, myths and spirit moving through those around me. Incarnational theology, lived through the stories about Jesus, presses me to live and to demonstrate spirit love. What now?

Spirit/Wisdom: Harlene you are ready to live the incarnation as shown in the stories about Jesus. You have never really conformed to this world's manifestation of spirit/wisdom, so heed my disciple Pope John XXII—show unity when necessary, offer freedom when in doubt, always love in all things, then will you become the transforming agent.

Self: I take that as a qualified yes–go public, but go slowly.

Sprit/Wisdom: Well, you can dare to risk, but do it in love. Beware of the arrogance of the right and perfect way, in humility, offer. You may not always succeed, but continue in the assurance you have discerned my will for the new age.

Self: My theme will be from Ephesians 3:21

"…to him who by the power at work within us is able to do far more abundantly than all that we ask or think" (July 1997).

Sacred Place of Body Movement

Hatha Yoga has taught me many things about spirituality. It has given me the combination of physical strength, mental alertness, spiritual nurture, and the yin-yang of caring for my whole self. It is the practice of integrating body, mind and spirit, knit together with the yarn of breathing. In the Hebrew language the word *ruach*, meaning spirit, is the same word that is used for breath, or wind. Consciously breathing in and breathing out gives focus to the mind, which sends a stabilizing message to the body. *Ruach* embraces the whole flow of the movement within any one yoga pose. I began taking instruction in yoga the day after I retired. It was my physical invigoration; it offered a different community of supportive friends; it stimulated my mind; but of prime importance to me, it fed my spiritual life. Today, the practice of yoga continues to be the major influence on my daily routine.

In the classes I have attended in many and various yoga studios over the last thirteen years, all the instructors have started with a comment like this one:

There is no perfect pose, just the pose that is perfect for you today. Whatever your body is telling you today is just what your body needs for today. There are always options if your body is not up to doing the pose in this session. Rest in 'child's pose' or 'downward dog' whenever you feel it is necessary. At another practice your body may feel differently.

This instruction is freeing, relaxing, liberating; it invites the student to release tension, to open, and to put aside any competitive tendencies. Likewise, yoga instructors end the class or the practice using similar methods: participants are asked to lie down on our yoga mats, cover up with a blanket or warm clothing, close our eyes and enter a 7-10 minute rest period. There can be quiet music playing, or sometimes a guided meditation alters our focus for this quiet time. We are slowly brought out of the rest, and in the final pose, we are seated in any position on the floor. Returning to breathing in and breathing out, we exhale with a long *ooooooommmmmm* called *OM*. An intention for peace is voiced by repeating the Sanskrit word *Shanti, Shanti, Shanti.*

Remembering my cathedral forest and the silence of that final walk in the wintertime, I am grateful for the privilege of finding holy ground and for the opportunity of naming my sacred places. As the yoga theme suggests, whatever my heart is telling me today is just what my spiritual nurturing needs for today. There is no perfect place, no how or where or when to name a sacred place of nurturing. Taking away the pressure of 'should', 'must' and 'orthodoxy' has opened me to a multitude of sacred places. Each option has been a symbol; each symbol has pointed me to the indwelling holiness of my being.

Personal Notes and Reflections

From My Journal

Holy, Sacred, Presence

Holy, holy, holy,
merciful and mighty,
God in three persons,
Blessed Trinity.
(Heber, ca. 1820)
Holy, holy, holy,
All the world adores you,
God in creation,
Blessed Trinity.
(ca. 1990 H.W.)
Holy, holy, holy,
All the world surrounds me,
Love in its mystery
Blessed harmony.
(ca. 2000 H.W.)
Body, mind, and spirit,
Holy sacred presence,
All in creation,
Blessed harmony.
(Feb. 2013 H.W.)

My Cathedral

Holy forest cathedral
hemlock, cedar, fir trees,
decked in four seasons
blessed home of awe.
Holy forest cathedralanthems sung by nature,
birds, wind and trees makesacred music sounds.

Holy flora fauna
quietly add beauty, insects and animals
share in your presence.
Deep well of my centre
come transforming presence, sacred expression
blessed mystery
April, 2013

Ground of my Being

When all around me is chaotic,
when doing enters and controls me,
when caring overwhelms my being,
you are my centre, hub of silence.

                                        Nov. 2011

Personal Notes and Reflections

SHARING THE TRAIL

My perspective of the forest has definitely altered; I walk down the trail away from the trees on my mountainside. Creation will usher me into fresh natural settings; there will be new-found environment to hold my new-found faith. Yes, I lament the decaying ancient cedars as bearers of lost majesty; and yes, I rejoice in the nursing trees as bearers of new life. Only the essential quality of presence remains. It is time to leave this sacred cathedral.

I bike to a park; at other times, when I have walked the urban trails, I have noticed they share at least one thing in common with the forest trails. Painted on the paved walkway or nailed onto a post beside the dirt path, is the sign 'share the trail.' Whether it is the city seawall beside the ocean or the village Valley Trail among the trees, skateboarders, cyclists, rollerbladers, joggers, runners, parents with strollers and adults with walkers compete for space. All are reminded to share the trail, pets included.

Bulldozed trees, and one-way roads make routes for busloads of tourists; restaurants, playgrounds, swimming pools, his/her washrooms with running water, and souvenir shops shout out the change: from a secluded cathedral forest, to a public playground. But all of this busyness is on the circumference of a wooded area. Its centre still retains the quiet growth of wild flora and fauna; admittedly, I struggle to hear and to feel the quiet of their presence. A clump of ancient cedars remains, an amphitheatre caters to a theatre under the stars, a recent hurricane has blown down trees which continue their process of decaying and birthing. Life is vibrant. Beauty and spirituality can be in the vision of the beholder.

MOVING BEYOND

Integration: An Unlikely Image

A memoir asks unexpected questions about the meaning of life, provides unconventional answers, enlightening meditation, and hopefully opens the writer as well as the readers to new ways of thinking about life. This memoir of reflective images, writings and evolving ideas has cast fresh light on many of the byways and pathways that led me into contemporary 21st century spirituality. In the late '70s, at the time when thoughts of becoming an ordained minister were pregnant in my mind, I attended an introductory workshop on a type of meditation called visualization.

We were asked to sit with both feet on the floor, hands on our laps and eyes closed. The facilitator then guided us into our favourite spot in nature. Back then, my favourite place was an ocean beach on a hot day. Gradually, through her direction, we were to find a comfortable place, a rock, a log, and to settle into the quiet. This prompted me to shift spots to a boulder near a stream. She continued. "You see a man walking toward you; he wants to come and sit beside you and have a chat. You recognize this man; he is Jesus."

And then the shock came. I couldn't talk to this Jesus because I visualized him dressed in a pair of jeans and an old shirt! I kept trying to dress and re-dress him; Jesus needed to be in a white flowing gown, have a permanent smile on his face and long hair. I stopped listening to the suggestions from the guiding voice. It just wasn't working. My vision of Jesus was friendly, but he looked like any beach bum or hiker walking beside a stream. I guess after all of these years, I could say that birthing an image of Jesus has been a passion. In a visualization of him at my age now, he would probably appear bald and pushing a walker!

Integration: Fifth time meeting Jesus — once more, ca. 2013

After 25 years of wandering the wilderness in the 'land of don't know,' I remembered back to 1980, that first New Testament class and the 'red letter bible' professor. In subsequent classes, he often described himself as a *fundamentalist* Christian, not a *literalist* Christian. That is, he believed in the fundamental truth of the biblical narratives but not the literal truth of the story. At that time I didn't pay much attention to the distinction; I was getting used to his ability to shock.

(The shock factor was his use of the word 'fundamentalist.' Then, as it is now, a fundamentalist Christian is popularly known to be one who has a very narrow, exclusive, factual interpretation of the bible. Our professor was not such a person; he was pulling our leg(s). His use of the word fundamentalist was the more formal academic version of the word, rather than the populist.)

Now, decades later, through spiritual evolution, I recalled his statement. Again, I met Jesus just as though it was the first time. As a fundamentalist Christian, Lloyd, my professor, was a believer in the Christian mythology of stories. It was another *aha* moment he gave to the class. I discovered that this professor, Lloyd Gaston, theologian and teacher at the Vancouver School of Theology, had contributed more to my spiritual development than I could ever have imagined.

A Thesaurus lists these synonyms:

fundamental– essential, vital, deep, ultimate, underlying, as the underlying truth;

literal — accurate, exact, factual, honest, and straightforward, as the factual truth.

There is a story in the Gospel According to St. John that tells of Jesus speaking to a Samaritan woman at the community well while she is drawing a pail of water. Jesus, a Jew and a male, had broken two of the 1st century cultural codes: men did not speak to women in public and Jews did not speak to foreigners. Christian literalists might consider this an accurate account: physically there was a well in the countryside, a woman from Samaria, a man called Jesus, and they could quote the factual conversation between them. Christian fundamentalists might say that the conversation between a man and a woman in public or between a Jew and a Samaritan in 1st century Judea was taboo and would not have happened unless the narrative was meant to convey an underlying truth. For them, it tells the fundamental truths that a) a woman is a person worthy of conversation, b) all people may interact in public, and c) people from different ethnic backgrounds may speak to each other freely. Exclusion is out; men and women and foreigners do not have to be separated.

Or, there is the wilderness story of Jesus. For forty days and forty nights, Jesus lived in the wilderness reflecting on his own spirituality. While he was there, the devil tempted him three times, pressing Jesus to follow him and to rebuke God. Again, the literalists might quote the exact conversations Jesus had with the devil. The devil as presented here is an honest straightforward portrayal of a competing, evil god, one to fear, one who would do harm. Again, the fundamentalist might say that it was a narrative of ultimate truth, that we all have temptations to face. We are given choices to do right or wrong according to the morals and ethics of the culture and society's current laws, to do the good suggested by our positive wisdom or to do the evil suggested by our negative potential. There was no physical wilderness, no god-devil. We create our own wilderness times, our own harm–addiction, abuse, anger, violence. Every man, every woman, is called to spend time listening and reflecting on situations of temptation and to choose a positive or negative response.

Jesus is the name of the male character in these stories of ultimate truth. It took me a long time to meet a Jesus like this. He is a parable of god and paradigm of humanity (Sechillebeeckx), an archetypal character pointing to the divinity in each person (Harper), and a symbol of fundamental truth (Gaston). The narratives about Jesus were written as parables of imagined events to typify spiritual or moral relations, allegories of meaningful symbolic representations;

fundamentally-speaking, they are myths: ultimate truth, underlying the essential experience in human spirituality. I can say that Jesus is the ultimate sacred symbol pointing me to the mystery of a holy spiritual presence.

Integration: Biblical Stories

Biblical stories understood from the fundamentalist's point of view offer universal human truths about life, the mystery of spirituality, and our place in this world. This revelation, that Jesus is a symbol of sacred presence, affirmed the spiritual myth for me. Mythologist Joseph Campbell clearly tells us about myths in *The Pagan Christ*:

The deepest truths about life, the soul, personal meaning, our place in the universe, our understanding, and the mystery we call God can be described only by means of a story (mythos) or ritual drama. The myth is fictional, the timeless truth it expresses is not (Harper, 2004, p. 17).

By definition, a spiritual myth is fictional ~ a legend, a fairy tale, a saga, a parable, or an allegory ~ expressing a timeless sacred truth.

Reading and reflecting on this description, confirmed by many authors, triggered my interest in the idea of a Christian mythology. Because Christianity was born when Greek mythology was popular, a Christian myth can tell a spiritual truth. Most mainline Christian scholars would tell us that the Christmas stories of the Virgin conception, the wise men following a star, the angels singing to the shepherds, and the birth in a manger in Bethlehem, are not facts of history, but they can be stories of truth. These stories are the authors' attempts to understand the powerful impact myths had on their lives. They told the mythos through a man, a woman, a baby, wise men, and shepherds with whom their gods connected.

For me, a spiritual myth is a story about relationship: the ordinary experiences of joy, love, kindness, gentleness, sharing, pain, suffering and, the truth and values encountered in one's secular life that intersects with the holy mystery experienced in one's spiritual life. Myths are symbolic narratives pointing to one's personal story or the culture's story; they are powerful. For instance, when I celebrate

Christmas, I want to listen to the story with new ears: this Nativity myth tells me that holy wisdom and the spirit of love are born in every human being. I listen with spiritual ears to the mythical stories of Easter; they speak of deep and ultimate truths. The crucifix represents death by suffering. When heard mythically instead of literally, the crucifix as a sacred symbol points beyond the story to a profound truth about suffering and pain in our world and the unavoidability of death. The empty cross represents the resurrection. The empty cross as a sacred symbol points beyond the story, and, when heard mythically rather than literally, reveals an insightful truth about healing, hope, new life. In life, in death, in life after life, we are not abandoned.

Now every time I read the stories about the biblical spiritual leaders ~ Abraham, Moses, David, Jesus, Paul, Sarah, Leah, Miriam, Ruth, Mary, Elizabeth and Lydia ~ their stories ask of me: Who do you say that I am? These stories are not literal facts of the character's life but fundamental truths of what can happen to each of us and for each of us.

Integration: The Face of Compassion

A long time ago, I left the home of the maple tree woodlots and wandered in the land of 'don't know'. Here I am, almost back home to trees, only it is urban streets that are lined with trees, deciduous maple trees. As I suspected, since the Cathedral gave me the tree as my holy symbol, the maple has become a new holy symbol, and for a different arena of sacredness.

I propose to introduce into this new land of learning my conception of a sacred symbol for letting go. The idea for creating my sacred symbol came from Christina Feldman's book *Compassion–Listening to the Cries of the World* (2005). The symbol is the seed of the hardwood maple tree, called by the locals a maple key. It is the symbol of the maple key that adorns the text in the section, From My Journal. The seed, really two adjoining seeds about the size of two small green peas, has two wings, one for each seed. This symbol, this seed-with-wings, for me points to the sacredness of letting go; the seed points to compassion; the wings point to wisdom and patience. Anyone can find this sacred symbol in the Garden of Compassion.

Seed-with-wings, the winged key to wisdom-compassion-patience, twirls into the interior of self and buries itself deeply within our waiting soil. In the Garden of Compassion, it is nurtured by rich, healthy soil, fertilized with softness, watered with love, and cultivated with healing to bring forth the blooms of the heart: openness, calm, empathy, acceptance, tolerance, and loving kindness. In this nurturing climate, the growth of compassion encourages the mind to face its fears: helplessness, anger, suffering, and hurt existing on the shadow side of self.

Softening, Opening, Accepting

Letting go was my first step to compassionate living–to have compassion for myself, for others, and for my church. The letting go as I named it in Chapter 2 allowed my heart to soften, to open, and to accept. Once I let go of my agitation, frustration and inward suffering, there was room for patience and wisdom ~ the two wings on the seed of compassion. Grieving the separation from orthodox Christianity was similar to grieving the loss of my family members. It took time; there was denial, anger, agitation, resistance, fear, doubt, blame, helplessness. With the knowledge of chaos and re-formation, finally, came acceptance and liberation.

Recognizing my inability to change the root cause of my spiritual anxiety, I discovered an inner power: the ability to be present, to hear wisdom, to accept patience, and to be embraced by compassion. I was not striving to move up a ladder to spiritual perfection, not reaching the next hierarchal level of faith development; I didn't even think about moving to the next coloured segment in the spirituality membrane of evolution. Spiritual evolution came to me as a consequence of the quest: questioning, risking, experimenting, thinking, feeling, and listening. The previously unknown spirituality took on its own shape and form.

When I slowly released myself from trying to do something to alleviate the outward ferment, the inner ferment disappeared. As the literature says, learning compassionate caring of self is the only way to have compassionate caring for others. I am aware, in a different way, of those in isolation, sorrow, grief, and despair. To care for others, to show compassion, is to accept the hurt in the world and to help relieve the pain only where it is possible for me to act. By softening, opening, and accepting, I was able to expand my understanding of compassion. I journaled:

All of life is letting go; all of living is about changing; all will disappear: birth–death, appear–disappear, come–go, all will pass. The fundamental reality is, that nothing is permanent; controlling to hang on to loved ones, to things, to places, to creeds, is an exercise in futility. To disregard this essential premise of life is to invite suffering into my life. Letting go brought freedom to discover, as well as to realize that the process will be repeated continually for as long as I live (May, 2013).

Strangely, I found business communities revamping their vocabulary, responding to the spiritual hunger that was evident even within their surroundings. At one time in the '80s, Ross returned to Vancouver after attending the Board of Directors' meeting in Toronto. He told me about their plan to design a company mission statement. I was surprised that they would use the word mission which was associated with church language. He replied, 'If you have a good word, you might as well use it.' After that, I kept tuned for other good churchy words within the workplace. I observed that in the '90s the corporate world adopted the word 'spirit' to identify the culture of their workplace; in the 2000s that population's chosen word was soul. The mission, spirit, and soul of business organizations had changed their culture. Spirituality was re-forming in new places, particularly outside of the religious communities. With my passion for using non-traditional language for faith and spirituality and witnessing traditional words being used in a post-theistic context, I mentally assigned faith and spirituality to metamorphosis in a chrysalis.

Years later and during the writing of this memoir, the evolution and transformation of faith and spirituality within the chrysalis emerged, as heart-wisdom soulality. The innovative power that brought forth the sacred symbol of compassion had created a new word: **soulality** *soul/al/ity* n. 1. of soul quality; sacredness within; 2. proceeding from faith and spirituality; concerned with the sacred, emotional, intellectual, parts of all humans.

I thought: I have just given post-theism a new word.

Integration: Circles of Healing

Sharing the faith-life trail took me to spiritual freedom. Here the sky was big, the land almost flat, and I was drawn to circles of sharing and healing. Until now the walk had been linear, one-directional, moving forward in the search for answers to my questions. After all this, I have found it to be true that ~ just as my life is grounded in my home, but I am not stuck in the house, or my parenting is grounded in family, but I am not stuck in the traditional family model ~ my faith is grounded in Christianity, but I am not stuck in religion. And so, discovering this new pathway back to my faith-home, through crowded park, and busy ocean beach and on a trail shared with everyone, I began to walk with other fellow travelers. On spiritual trails together, we nourished our spirits. Poised in the reality of a new faith dawning within spirituality, I waited.

I have experienced a change of heart through yoga and other modalities: psychological counseling, contemplation, reading–reflect-ing-responding, Healing Touch, and spiritual healing. Being alert to 'spiritual healing' was a new idea for me. I took a course that included a series of spiritual healing meditations, given by Lyn, who is a spiritual healer. She is wise in the ways of auras and moving energy. During her sessions, we all learned to sense our auras and acknowledge their boundaries and to meditate from the core of our being. She called it 'running your energy.' Journal:

The experience: I began to feel my energy and to acknowledge that the energy comes from my spirit, not from my body hence, I am a spiritual being.

The healing: Three healers came to assist Lyn and each one in the class was given the opportunity to receive a healing. Moving energy to flow without obstruction they cleared the pathways, and energy moved at each of the 7 chakras.

The insight: After the healing, I sat alone and felt a deep sense of gratitude-peace of the day. I silently prayed, "This woman is grateful," which did surprise me because normally I might have responded with the traditional, "Thank you God." Immediately I recognized another spiritual paradigm conversion in my prayer life. Lyn came and sat down beside me to debrief the healing. I said that I was fine; I had nothing to heal–thinking in terms of my body–but told her about my spiritual experience with the words in my prayer. She gave me her definition of healing–'to move.' I had experienced a spiritual healing. There was a moving, a shift in my prayer life. I have experienced my first spiritual healing. (March 2004).

I practiced living, in Lyn's terms, with the bubble or aura of love surrounding me, which would give me the strength to carry on. Strangely, I found this most helpful when playing duplicate bridge. Looking across the bridge table at a strong, aggressive, opponent, I tried thinking to myself, 'I am surrounded by my bubble of love.' It worked. I bid the hand and played much more confidently. In other words, I took responsibility for my own feelings, and, I was not intimidated.

Upon reflection, I know now that I have had several spiritual healings that have come during my contemplative moments: reading, reflecting, responding. The first change of heart occurred when I was in my 40s when I was working through my relationship with my mother, as often happens in maturation. I attended a daylong retreat at Cenacle House in Vancouver. With Mom on my mind, I took the biblical story of Moses and Pharaoh in which Pharaoh's heart was hardened and he refused to let Moses' people go. Then in my prayer/reflection time I wrote, 'harden not my heart against my Mom.' I also created a mantra, 'harden not my heart.' I grew. I changed. My spirit energy moved into openness and acceptance.

Actually, my journal provides many examples. At one time, over a period of sessions with a psychologist, and again on silent retreats, I reflected on and dealt with my relationship with different family members. What all of the sessions had in common was that I went into the activity of listening, praying, and counseling fully expecting the other to be changed! Well, that didn't happen; it was I who changed. Every time, it was about me changing. After the exercise, I saw myself quite differently in relationship with each person; I was able to be open to change and to accept the shift in me. Spiritual healing led to a new relationship with each one.

Integration: Beyond

As a storyteller I have found the language of the metaphor a helpful tool to explain the evolution of my faith journey. The nursing tree welcomes all to its site of incubation: moss, wild flowers, coniferous and deciduous seeds receive its nurture. If you look at the photo on the cover of this book, you will see that it is the coniferous tree that gives birth to both the maple and evergreen seedlings.

In the first millennium, the Judaic covenantal message of love became the nursing tree for the Jesus group of men and women. The growth of that 'Jesus movement' became the covenantal message of unconditional love called Christianity. In this second millennium, Christianity's message of unconditional love could become the nursing tree that births harmonious love to disenchanted Boomers and Millennials.

In fairy tales, sagas, legends and, yes, in Christian myths, to find fundamental truth, the hero had to leave the nest. Jesus, born into a Hebraic/Jewish family left home for several years and walked the countryside telling his story. When he returned home he saw his world differently. His religious and spiritual life nurtured a new spirituality. Centuries later it became imbedded in the religion called Christianity.

Born in the Christian era, I practiced professional ministry in a post-Christian context, and now I live in the post-theistic milieu. Perhaps an evolved spirituality and faith in the Jesus of mythology rests in gestation within the chrysalis. A transformed spirituality may emerge, butterfly-like, offering communities a yet-unidentified-message of universal love, but for this in-between time, I offer soulality.

This memoir is about the adventures that came to me when I did leave my familial religious training. Venturing into the Cathedral Forest I found the mythological truths in stories about Jesus and other biblical spiritual leaders. I made my way into the spiritual labyrinth, whose centre of power encouraged me to create the Garden of Compassion; here the maple key symbol points me to the sacred wisdom and patience of compassion.

Crossing the threshold of the labyrinth, I stepped away from the religion of Christianity, into heart- wisdom soulality, sacred centre deep within. This metaphoric platform will hold, while crossing thresholds encountered by a continually evolving faith in the land of 'don't know'.

From My Journal

Spirit Energy

Spiritual healing unloosens.
Spiritual moving evokes.
Divine Energy enters.
Holy Mystery
Ground of Being
Experienced.
This woman is grateful.
Namaste
Shantih, Shantih, Shantih
Peace Peace Peace.
                    October, 2004

Fountain of Wisdom

Gushing strongly up my spine
Flowing firmly around my bones
Cascading gently over my cells
Caressing smoothly through my heart
Pulsating quickly into my mind;
Enthusing my soul with thoughts of gentleness
Impacting my spirit with will to move
Gracing me with actions of love
Wisdom impacts my spirit,
Willing me to move on.
                    Nov. 2012

Table Grace

In a world full of potential
May we be an instrument for transformation.
In a world full of abundance
May we be mindful of balance.
In a world full of beauty
May we see through joyful eyes.
Amen
    Sept. 2012

The Garden of Compassion

Virtual garden hidden deep
a universal cellular mass
an open heart and mind
unfolding the sacred seed ~
you are wisdom-compassion-patience.
Weeds sprout,
pity   bitterness
ignorance   anger   blame   isolation
despair separation
pain   hurt.
Accept weeds, impossible to stop them
accept weeds, they cannot be ignored.
Aware–wholeheartedly face fear, helplessness
listen–embrace adversity, suffering, pain.
To cultivate patient loving kindness
every person needs nurturing care.
In the garden, receive, stay present in the moment.
You are in the garden of compassion:
sacred wisdom-compassion-patience.
    May, 2013

Personal Notes and Reflections

EMBRACING THE ROAD AHEAD

My Forest Cathedral is now far behind me and I have moved on. It remains to embrace the next sojourners. The trees will welcome those new hikers, offering thin but sturdy branches for their walking sticks.

The trail for this spiritual journey began from my home, the home of my childhood. The trail, at this stage of the spiritual journey, ends in our home, the home of my sagehood. Like home, the transformation of my faith-life has taken place within the base camp of Christianity and its spiritual trails. For both Ross and me, home, family, and faith have always been priorities.

Today, my home has sidewalks into children's play areas and trails leading to the city's canal, and I sit on a bench in the park beside beds of multi-coloured tulips and well-pruned rose gardens. However, as I embrace the road ahead, I rest in the knowledge that circles of soul friends, support from family, and guidance from the holy mystery within will enable me to continue to grow toward wholeness and to continue on the spiritual path that I have created from the deep well of spirit-wisdom, ground of my being.

"There is a calm place of embracing the road."

Kashi Richardson: My first yoga teacher and now friend, in conversation at my kitchen counter.

(August, 2012)

EPILOGUE

"Five years ago, it was the Spiritual Directors International conference in Chicago, in the middle of Joyce Rupp's workshop on "Return From Exile, Bringing My Soul Home," that I heard the voice in my soul cry out.

I listened. I cried. I cried. I left her workshop. I walked the streets of Chicago. In my hotel room, I answered the phone and heard Ross say, 'Cam died this week'; the son of my soul was dead.

Cam had returned to his origin, from his place of exile in this world." (April, 2010)

"The week of Cam's agony I was in Chicago at an SDI conference. Two of my four nights there, my spirit would not settle. I got out of bed and wrote a myth of the love-spirit tree. I thought that my restless spirit was birthing the myth, but even after writing it, I could not sleep. The second night was just as restless; a rash had developed on my chest. Needing my sleep I got up, and that time I took a Tylenol. The third day in a group session, I cried. I could actually feel my body rise from abdomen to chest and I felt exhausted, but released and calm.

After Ross told me about Cam's passing over I believe that his death might have occurred at the time of my release. I haven't heard about the details since I am still in the Toronto airport." (April 04, 7:00 a.m. 2005)

From My Journal

The Lovespirit Tree

A long time ago when the planet Earth was young and the creator had put human life on Earth, the Creator-god made a very special tree called Lovespirit. This tree grew coloured circles of fruit on its branches. There were small purple circles, medium-sized red circles, and huge blue circles. Every circle was different, tiny dots on a pink circle, yellow smiles on a black circle, even a gold and green one, and deep chocolate brown!

Lovespirit grew big and strong; it had so many healthy circles. One day Creator-god noticed how many people liked to hang out close to Lovespirit. They laughed together, shared their stuff, helped each other, and had picnics under the big blue circles. They were joyful. They treated each other with kindness, respect, gentleness, and patience. It was a safe place to be. Creator-god said, "Lovespirit you have such a good influence on these people. I want everyone on Earth to enjoy your coloured circles of fruit. I will put the tree called Lovespirit into every baby boy and every baby girl who is born in Antarctica, Africa, Asia, Europe, North America, South America and Australia. Creator-god named the colourful circles. Big blue was called **love**, small purple was **kindness**, middle-sized red became **patience**, the pink with tiny dots **hope**, happy black with its smiles was **joy**, gold and green was named **faith** and deep chocolate brown was **wisdom**. Lovespirit grew these circles of values in every body.

Now everyone who lives on planet Earth has an inner Lovespirit tree. All of the girl babies and all of the boy babies can choose to let the Lovespirit tree grow strong and healthy to produce lots of fruit circles of value called, love, joy, kindness, patience, hope, faith and wisdom. And it is so today in the whole wide world of planet Earth. (Thursday, March 31st — April 1st, 2005).

APPENDIX

References

Biblical & Hymn Citations

Good News Bible The Bible in Today's English Version, (1976). New York, NY: Thomas Nelson Publishers.

Co-Chairs Nancy E. Hardy and Leonard Lythgoe, Hymn and Worship Resource Committee of the United Church of Canada, *Voices United The Hymn and Worship Book of the United Church of Canada*.(1996). Toronto, ON: The United Church Publishing House.

Works Cited

Bridges, Wm. (2004). *Transitions: Making Sense of Life's Changes.* Cambridge, MA: Da Capo Press.

Funk, Robert. (1993). *The Five Gospels: The Search for the Authentic Words of Jesus.* New York, NY: Simon and Schuster.

Harper, Thomas. (2004). *The Pagan Christ: Recovering the Light.* Toronto, ON: Thomas Allen.

Hawking, Lucy & Hawking, Stephen. (2011). *George and the Big Bang.* New York, NY: Simon & Schuster Books for Young Readers.

Heber, Reginald. *Holy, holy, holy, lord God almighty*, (poem ca.1820). *Voices United*. (1996).

Mabry, J. R. Generational Ministry: Spiritual Guidance for the Five Adult Generations Alive Today. *Presence An International Journal of Spiritual Direction.* 18, no.4 (Dec.2012): 13- 22. Bellevue, WA: Spiritual Directors International.

Michener, James. (1965). *The Source: A Novel.* New York, NY: Random House Trade Paperbacks.

Newman, Peter, C. "Change Demands Inspired Leadership." *Maclean's Canada's National Magazine.* (Nov.08, 2004): 26. Toronto: Rogers Publishing Ltd.

O'Murchu, Diarmuid. (1998). *Reclaiming spirituality: A new spiritual framework for today's world.* New York, NY: The Crossroad Publishing Company.

Rohr, Richard.(2009). *The Naked Now: Learning to See as the Mystics See.* New York, NY: The Crossroads Publishing Company.

Robinson, John A.T. (1963). *Honest to God.* London, UK: SCM Press Ltd.

Rupp, Joyce. (1990). *Dear heart come home: The path to midlife spirituality.* New York, NY: Crossroad Publisher.

_____, 1996.Stars in my heart. *"The Star in my heart Experiencing sophia, inner wisdom."* San Diego,CA: Lura Media.

Spong, J.S. (2001). *A new Christianity for a New World: WhyTtraditional Faith is Dying and How a New Faith is being Born.* San Francisco CA: Harper San Francisco.

Schilibeeckx, Edward. (1979). *Jesus, an experiment in Christology.* Translation: Hubert Hoskins. New York, NY: A Crossroads Book The Seabury Press.

The First Letter of Paul to the Corinthians, I Cor.13.4-8.) (1952). *The Holy Bible Revised Standard Version.* New York, NY: Thomas Nelson.

Tillich, Paul. (1963). *The Eternal Now.* New York, NY: Scribner's Sons.

_____, (1957). *The Courage to Be.* New Haven MA: Yale University Press.

_____, (1955). *The New Being.* New York, NY: Scribner.

Wesleyan Quadrilateral. (n. d.). In Wikipedia The free encyclopedia online. Retrieved

from http://en.wikipedia.org/wki/ Wesleyan_Quadrilateral#References

INTERACTING WITH THE MEMOIR

You too have a story to tell. Asking questions helps to connect you with your story; you can begin to notice, to become aware, and to name which experiences have been energizing and life-giving for you. The following steps are designed to help you describe in detail the specific experiences by which you have been most enlivened, those that have been energy-draining or unwelcome. These may be the areas in which you may want to "go deeper."

Your Memoir Journal can be any note book; it is always your private space to be shared only when you choose to do so. Incidentally, these steps may be used for any piece of literature upon which you choose to reflect.

Here are the 5 Steps for personal interacting with the memoir and the theme of each chapter:

1. Begin: to start, make an intention that is just for this particular time. For example, "today may I relax into my story"; or, "may I hear the wisdom that is right for me at this time."

2. Re-Read: From the chapter themes below, choose one chapter: What sub-title(s) within that chapter beckons you? Read it over.

3. Reflect: Spend time thinking about the ideas given in the section you have chosen. What is significant or unclear for you in your life? Is this your land of 'don't know'? What is helpful or challenging?

4. Respond: In your Personal Memoir Journal, write, draw, jot down, or doodle. What do you want to remember? What are your desires?

5. Complete: To end this section of your story, write an affirmation in one or two sentences in blank verse, rhyme, or prayer.

Chapter Themes

1. Courage to Grow — naming your personal and spiritual growth

2. Letting Go — moving on

3. Paradigm Shift — living in the difference

4. Appropriate Questions — for you personally and you culturally

5. Twenty-five Years in the Wilderness — wandering through past unsettledness and changes in your life

6. Naming Holy Ground — identifying your sacred experiences, places, and space

7. Moving Beyond — integrating your spirituality with the universal stories

About the Author

With her spirit-centred leadership, Harlene Walker founded the Workplace Centre for Spiritual and Ethical Development in 1986 in the heart of the Vancouver business district, where it continues to operate. Her team initiated the Vancouver Conference: Ethics in Business, and partnered with VanCity Savings Credit Union to create the Ethics in Action awards dinner. She was the first female chaplain to the Vancouver City Police Department and was nominated for the Vancouver YWCA Women of Distinction Award.

In her ministry, she practiced seeing old truths in new ways, fostered ecumenically based and multi-faith events, and offered spiritual guidance, silent retreats and innovative change. A guiding imperative in her ministry was to seek contemporary interpretations of the literature about spirituality and sacred experiences.

An ordained minister in the United Church of Canada, she has worked in congregational settings, was elected President of the B.C. Conference of the United Church of Canada, and Chair of the Vancouver-Burrard Presbytery. Now retired, she lives with her husband in Ottawa, Canada.

Crossing the Threshold, Metaphors of an Evolving Faith is her first book.

Printed in Canada